EX · LIBRIS

CAT

Somewhere There Is Still a Sun

SOMEWHERE THERE IS STILL A SUN

MICHAEL GRUENBAUM
with TODD HASAK-LOWY

Aladdin

New York   London   Toronto   Sydney   New Delhi

ALADDIN

An imprint of Simon & Schuster Children's Publishing Division
1230 Avenue of the Americas, New York, New York 10020
First Aladdin hardcover edition August 2015
For information about special discounts for bulk purchases,
please contact Simon & Schuster Special Sales at 1-866-506-1949
or business@simonandschuster.com.
The Simon & Schuster Speakers Bureau can bring authors
to your live event. For more information or to book an event
contact the Simon & Schuster Speakers Bureau at
1-866-248-3049 or visit our website at www.simonspeakers.com.
Jacket designed by Jessica Handelman
Interior designed by Mike Rosamilia
The text of this book was set in Goudy Oldstyle Std.
Manufactured in the United States of America 0715 FFG
2 4 6 8 10 9 7 5 3 1
Library of Congress Control Number 2014038660
Full CIP data is available from the Library of Congress.
ISBN 978-1-4424-8486-3 (hc)
ISBN 978-1-4424-8488-7 (eBook)

To the 1.5 million Jewish children who were killed during the Holocaust and specifically to all the Nesharim, not just to the few who survived, but to all the boys who lived with me in Room 7 in the school building L417 during my two-and-a-half-year incarceration in the Terezin concentration camp in Czechoslovakia, many of whom were much more talented than I am and unfortunately most of whose lives and contributions to society were cut short by being gassed on arrival in Auschwitz. And to our leader, Francis Maier, a.k.a. Franta, who at the age of twenty overcame the most unimaginably difficult circumstances and became a father to some eighty rambunctious boys, teaching them how to survive by forging a team spirit which has lasted until today.

—MICHAEL GRUENBAUM

To the Gruenbaum family, past, present, and future

—TODD HASAK-LOWY

Introduction

IN MAY 1945, A FEW DAYS AFTER WE WERE
liberated from the Terezin concentration camp, my mother
wrote the following letter to some relatives living abroad:

> *This is my first letter in which the threatening, indiscreet
> eyes of the censors do not know my thoughts. I do not
> know where to begin in order to describe to you (without
> leaving anything out) everything we lived through during
> the years since we last saw each other. Each card, each
> package from all of you was a bit of warmth, a bit of the
> happy surroundings that we lost. I am writing to you as I
> remember you, and yet we have the feeling here that we
> will never be able to find a bridge to those who have lived
> on the outside and who fortunately will never be able to
> grasp what horror, fear, and deep sorrow we experienced
> through the years just passed.*

We hardly have the hope of finding anyone [of our relatives alive]. We ourselves were saved by a miracle. We were collected for a transport three times and Misha even for a fourth time! You cannot imagine the contrasts between life and death. We look well even though nourishment was very inadequate. To illustrate this, I want to tell you that we—the three of us—consumed three eggs in two and a half years. All of which we procured secretly. They cost 170 crowns apiece. Misha's sister worked in the laundry, and Misha was a delivery boy—in place of a horse. He sometimes went to a friend with a notebook under his jacket to take some lessons, but it all failed because of the many obstacles and lack of time. We had to work ten hours a day.

We do not yet know how the future will shape up for us. None of our old friends are alive anymore. We do not know where we are going to live. Nothing! But somewhere in the world there is still a sun, mountains, the ocean, books, small clean apartments, and perhaps again the rebuilding of a new life.

What kind of place was my mother talking about? What kind of place forces a boy to work ten hours a day instead of going to school? What were "transports," and why was a miracle needed to keep us off them? And what was the miracle?

The book you are about to read answers these questions and many more. It's a book about my experiences from the ages of nine to fifteen, when the German Nazi army conquered Prague, my hometown, and then did their very best to wipe out Prague's Jewish community in its entirety. It's a story I only thought to tell the world when I was already an old man. Why did I wait seventy years to tell it? Well, that's a story in and of itself.

When my mother passed away in 1974, I inherited the album she assembled after the war, an album made out of the memorabilia she saved from Terezin. Terezin was a transition camp in northern Czechoslovakia to which most Jews from Czechoslovakia (and some Jews from other parts of Europe) were sent before they were later sent to Auschwitz for extermination.

For sentimental reasons I kept her album well preserved all these years. It wasn't until I also was reaching an "advanced age" that I decided to find a place that would take good care of it just as I did. I vacillated between the United States Holocaust Memorial Museum in Washington DC, the Ghetto Museum in Terezin in the Czech Republic, the Jewish Museum in Prague, and Beit Theresienstadt, the

kibbutz in Israel that collects and displays Terezin memorabilia. I decided to donate the album as well as my memory
book (in which many of my roommates in Terezin wrote
a commemorative page) to the United States Holocaust
Memorial Museum, because I felt it was a safe place and
they had the financial resources to preserve the two precious items in good condition for posterity.

Ms. Judith Cohen, one of the archivists from the
museum, came to my house and couldn't believe her good
fortune, because at this point the museum gets few such
donations. And I was giving her not just a document or
two, but an entire collection, all organized and well preserved. The museum was so elated with my donation that
it decided to dedicate an entire page in the museum's
2010 calendar to my mother and our family. Furthermore,
Ms. Cohen took a couple of pages from my mother's album
and arranged to have them included in the museum's per-
manent collection. Last, she made a short film for the
museum's Curators' Corner collection that summarized
our experiences under the Nazis. Incidentally, many of
these same documents have been reproduced in the book
you now hold.

The resulting excitement inspired me to write a picture book for children. In that original version of the story
I chose to have a bear narrate how our family avoided

being transported from Terezin to Auschwitz, and thus to our death in the gas chambers waiting there. If you want to know why I chose a bear for that story, you'll have to read this book; I promise you'll find the answer there. I wrote a children's story because I learned that there was a great demand for stories for this age. Also, many years ago I had written several stories spoken by various animals.

After writing that story, I started out on the long process of trying to get my story published, a process that involved many letters to many literary agents and publishers. In the end, no one wanted to publish what I had written. One of the several reasons I was given was that children who play with teddy bears are not ready age-wise to learn about the Holocaust, or children who are ready to learn about the Holocaust don't play with teddy bears anymore. So the feeling was that there was only a very small window of potential readers for such a children's story.

But, on the bright side, there was one publisher who wanted to know if I would be willing to work with another writer, a professional, to help tell my story for a middle-school audience, a suggestion I readily agreed to. What followed were another couple of years of working with one writer, and then another, until this book was produced. I must say that I'm very pleased with the results.

The book is an amazing example of one person's (my

mother's) courage, perseverance, ingenuity, resilience, and a strong desire to stay alive and hope that better times would eventually come. It took a while, but these times came, though they came on a different continent. After liberation in 1945 we settled back in Prague and tried hard to return to a normal life. But soon thereafter it started to look like the Communists were trying to take over the government. My mother, seeing the writing on the wall, wrote to friends in the United States to ask for visas for us. Six weeks after the official Communist takeover we left Czechoslovakia, but we had to wait in Cuba for two years before our quota number came up to enter the United States.

Just as my mother dreamed, we were able to success-fully rebuild our lives here. And we were rebuilding from almost nothing. On four separate occasions we lost all of our property. At first the Nazis confiscated whatever they could. We then lost what we tried to save by sending it to a warehouse in London that was later bombed by the Germans. We were able to take only one hundred pounds per person to Terezin. We got very few of our other posses-sions back from neighbors and friends when we returned from Terezin. And what we shipped to New York City before our departure from Czechoslovakia was eventually auctioned off because someone forgot to pay the monthly rent. So we had to start all over again each time, but what we learned was that material possessions are replaceable and, in the overall scheme of things, not important. Both my sister and I were able to find wonderful lifelong partners, build new families, and thus bring my mother much well-deserved happiness.

But you won't find a lot about that happiness in the story you hold in your hand. This book is about the hardest years of my life, years that were so hard they almost ended my life before I even reached my fifteenth year. Some of this has already been described in my late wife's book, *Nešarim: Child Survivors of Terezín* by Thelma Gruenbaum, which was published some ten years ago. But this is the first time it's being told for readers who are the age now that I was way back then. .

When people speak about the Holocaust these days, they often say "Never forget." I certainly agree with them, but before you can pledge to remember something, you have to *know* it to begin with. I'm hopeful that this book will serve as the kind of "bridge" my mother wrote about in that letter of hers from 1945. I believe that by reading this book you'll be able to understand the world we lived in—and nearly died in—from 1939 to 1945. And, if I had to guess, once you truly understand that world, you'll never forget it.

—Michael Gruenbaum

Part I

Prague, Czechoslovakia

March 11, 1939

MY RECORD IS FIFTEEN.

"Why are you rushing, Misha?" Father has been asking ever since we left our apartment. "Slow down," he kept telling me, nearly laughing, while we were walking along the river. The Vltava. The best river in the world.

He didn't know that I was warming up, getting ready. Because today is the day; I can feel it.

Father likes to take his time. "A person isn't supposed to rush on Shabbat," he's reminded me about five times already. But I can't blame him. He works so hard all week. I mean, he's barely even around most of the time. Some nights he doesn't come home at all. And he's going to London tomorrow, because of his work. I hate it when he's gone, but I guess when you're one of the lawyers for the richest family in Prague you do what they say.

But I have a job too. To break my record. Today.

We're almost at the bridge. The Cechuv. Seagulls are chasing each other along the river, playing their secret games. The castle pokes up at the sky like usual, high above everything. Maybe we can go up there once he gets back from his trip. See the changing of the guards and look at the city down below. I'll ask Father when he's not so annoyed with me.

We turn off the quay and onto the bridge, busy with people and cars. Excellent. Here comes Pavel Goren, our doctor. Who just so happens to have the biggest belly of any doctor anywhere. But why is he walking *away* from the Old-New Synagogue? Who cares, this is perfect. He'll distract father.

"Shabbat shalom, Pavel," my father says.

"Hello, Karl," Pavel says, and ruffles my hair, his stomach brushing against my ear. "Tell me something, Misha, have you been growing again?"

But I don't answer. Because the bridge is perfect right now. Old men and their canes. Girls chattering with their friends. A couple led by their dog.

"It's Madga; she's ill," Pavel tells my father. "Every year in March, it's the same thing."

I guess I'm supposed to care, but I have more important things to worry about. Plus, I'm sure of it, in a moment they'll be talking about Germany and Hitler and the Nazis, which is all any adult seems to talk about these days. So boring.

Three boys pass us. Bigger than me, but so what?

I'm off.

One of the boys says, "The next World Cup is ours. You'll see."

"No way," the tallest says. "Brazil will beat us. Again."

"Are you crazy?" the third boy says. "Oldrich is only getting better."

"You're both idiots," says the tall one. They stop to argue, pointing their fingers at each other.

Fine with me. I pass them.

One, two, three.

Next is an old man, shuffling along slowly. No problem.

Four.

And two women, one of them pushing a stroller. Unfortunately, babies don't count, but still.

Five, six.

Someday this will be an Olympic event. At least it should be. Prague will host the Olympics, and I'll be a national hero. *Gruenbaum's about to set a new mark! He's passing the German. Thirty-seven! Thirty-seven people passed on a single bridge! A new Olympic record!*

But okay, I've got to focus. And no running allowed. If you run and they catch you, you're disqualified.

Here's a family. Like ours. A boy and his sister. She looks about four years older than him, too, just like with us. I wonder if she tells him to stop acting like a baby all the time too. Doesn't matter, they're tossing bits of bread out to the seagulls.

Seven, eight, nine, ten.

Can't get distracted in the middle. Not by that boat sliding underneath. And not by the urge to turn back to see the old castle, even though it looks best from this spot. Because it's got to be the biggest castle anywhere. I swear, sometimes its four steeples—especially the tallest one at the top of the cathedral—they disappear right into the clouds.

"Michael Gruenbaum!" my father screams at me. "What are you doing?" I pretend I didn't hear him. He won't be that mad; my father almost never gets *that* mad. Another reason he's the best dad anywhere.

Here's a couple, holding hands. Piece of cake.

Eleven, twelve.

Four more and it's a record.

A woman walking her dog.

Thirteen.

Two men arguing in German. Walking fast, as if they know, as if they were sent here to discourage our nation's best bet. But it won't be so easy, gentlemen. My legs might be short, but my feet are quick.

Fourteen, fifteen!

I've tied my record.

Only there's just one problem. Oh no. There's no one left. And the end of the bridge, fast approaching, is barely fifty feet away.

Oh well, a tie is still impressive.

But what's this? Someone passing me!

A tall man, in shorts. Mother would say it's much too cold for shorts. And I have to agree, not that I'd say so. Gym shoes on his feet. Speeds past me. The bulge of a soccer ball in a bag on his back. I hear him huffing and see the sweat on his neck shining in the sunlight.

He must be a pro, or will be someday. Probably knows Antonin Puc personally. A striker if I had to guess.

But so what? Because I, Misha Gruenbaum (my parents only call me "Michael" when I'm in trouble), will one day represent Czechoslovakia in the Pass People on the Bridge event at the Olympics. It'll be a sport by 1948 or 1952, and by then I'll be in my prime.

So I begin to sprint, because here's a little known rule only the most dedicated competitors know: If someone else is running, you can run to pass them. That's allowed. Father won't be happy, me running like this in my clothes for synagogue. But so what? Someday, when the medal is hanging in our living room, when I'm a national hero, he'll understand it was all worth it.

Twenty feet to go. The man in the shorts turns his head, puzzled. Grins. Picks up his pace. But he's no match for a sprinter like Gruenbaum.

I break the finish line a moment before him!

The crowd goes wild!

The national anthem plays!

Sixteen!

A new record! I did it!!! Sixteen!!!

"Misha! Misha!"

I turn and hurry back to Father. Wipe the sweat off on the inside of my sleeves so he won't see. Try to get my breath back to normal.

"Look at the castle," I tell him. Because maybe that will distract him.

"Misha," he says, concerned. "You're only eight years old. You can't just run off like that. I couldn't even—"

"Can we go?" I ask, pointing past his shoulder.

"Go? What are you—"

"To the castle." Father opens his mouth, like he's about to say something. "The first Sunday after you get back, from London. Please."

He puts his *tallit* bag under his left arm and turns toward the castle. It worked; I can see it in his eyes. He forgets about everything. Maybe even those stupid Nazis he and the rest of the adults won't shut up about.

"Sure," he says quietly, still staring across the river. "I don't see why not." He puts his arm around me, and we continue along the bridge toward the synagogue. "So long as it doesn't rain."

My dad's like that. Always worrying a bit. As if something is always about to go wrong. But if he knew about my new record, he'd realize that things are only going to get better. Because sometimes I can just tell.

March 15, 1939

"MISHA, GET AWAY FROM THAT WINDOW already," Mother orders from the kitchen.

But I don't. I can't. Because it's not every day that an entire army marches right past your building.

First there were actual tanks. Dozens of them. Their treads whirring loudly, their cannons pointing straight ahead. And then the motorcycles with their sidecars. How I'd love to ride in one of those. Just not with a Nazi, of course. But with Father, definitely.

Only he's still in London, which is really unfair. Mother's here, but it's not the same, because she'd never drive a motorcycle. She did stand by the window with me for a few minutes, her hand on my shoulder, breathing deeply, like she was preparing to dive into a deep, deep lake. Then she shook her head and was gone.

Maybe it was when the people lining the streets started

saluting the motorcycles. The way Germans salute. Even some people in the balconies across the way were doing it. Arm straight, hand open, fingers together. The whole thing shooting out diagonally from your chest. Almost like when you really want the teacher to call on you in class. I've done it myself, just to try it out. In my room, with the door closed. Because Mother and Father would kill me if they saw.

I can hear her now. In the kitchen with Christina, her friend from down the street. Now that they've turned off the radio, I can hear that they're whispering about something. Even with all the noise from below.

And where is Marietta? Probably in her room reading. She acts like every other big sister, like she doesn't care about anything. But how can you not care about this? An entire army, probably the strongest one in the whole world, right outside our window.

Here come the soldiers. Hundreds and hundreds of them. Marching in perfect rectangles. Seven soldiers across, and probably twenty from front to back. Twenty at least. Giant marching rectangles. Too many to count. And just like everyone's arms when they salute, their legs are completely straight. The knees never bend. All their feet come up together, toes shooting straight out, the same foot at the same time. Up, down, up, down, up, down, up, down. Feet shooting out past their round metal helmets, which are dark, dull green. Almost gray even. And they don't seem to move, their helmets don't. Just like the guns resting on their shoulders don't move.

"Leci," I call her name, because I can hear her straightening out the living room, even though it's already clean. There's not much work for our nanny this afternoon, since I can tell Mother was straightening up nonstop from the second I went off to school this morning.

"Yes, Misha?"

I point down to the street. "What are those?" She comes over, bringing her Leci smell with her. Sugar and soap and something else I can never figure out.

"Those?" she asks, her long, thin face completely still.

"The shiny things sticking off the top of their guns. What are those?"

"Bayonets," she says. "Attached to their rifles, Misha."

"They look like knives," I say. "But why would you need a knife if you already have a rifle? Can you shoot with them attached like that? Do our soldiers have them too?"

Only she doesn't answer. She's gone. The soldiers keep marching down below. More and more people are saluting, like they're happy to have this huge army in our city. They've even stretched this giant red flag—I guess it's a banner—across part of the crowd. All red except for the white circle with the black swastika in the middle. It's a cloudy, cloudy day, but the red, it's still so bright. The Germans must be pretty organized if they remembered to bring flags and banners with all this other stuff, too.

"Misha," Leci says, back again, "have some." And she hands me a small plate of cookies. Stars and moons and swirls. I bet she could make a swastika-shaped cookie, not that I'd eat it. So weird, just handing me a plate of cookies like that. She knows I'm not allowed to eat out here. She's told me so herself a thousand times. Not that I'm about to say anything.

Then she's gone again. The house is so quiet. Did Christina leave? It would be weird if she did, because she always kisses me on both cheeks whenever she leaves, her light blond hair covering my entire face while she bends over. Mother must have gone to her room. That's okay, more cookies for me.

When will this parade end? How can there still be more soldiers coming? But no one outside is going anywhere. Not even the people in the balconies. And what is that one couple doing? Why are they standing on the outside of the railing? Even Jarek, the bravest boy in our class, wouldn't do something that crazy. Not five stories up from the street he wouldn't. No way.

They're holding hands. Which leaves them only one hand to keep hold of the railing. My mouth opens to call out for Mother, but something keeps me from making a sound. And it's not the half-eaten cookie in my mouth.

Only the edges of their feet are still on the balcony's ledge. What are they doing? Why don't they get down?! C'mon, don't be stupid, get off of there already!

They jump.

They jump!

Or did they just let go? Doesn't matter, because now they're in the air, his hat flying off immediately, her dress opening up. Like a parachute. Only it's much too small. It's not going to save her, and she's not going to save him. They're falling so fast, even though their bodies slowly turn to the side at the same time. They're falling!

I push my face right up to the window to see, but my breath immediately fogs up everything. So I run around to a different window, on the other side of the couch, only I trip on the edge of the coffee table. My elbow hits the floor hard, and suddenly I get this feeling that I made the whole thing up, because why would anyone jump off a balcony? Even if the Nazis are really mean, how could you just decide to jump, because what could be worse than jumping straight to the ground from that high? My eyes must be fooling me.

So I get back up, but I can't decide where to go, because the smart thing to do would be to go get Mother. Especially if that couple really jumped, especially if they're lying flat on the ground right now. I don't want to think what will happen if I look and see them there, maybe with blood coming out from wherever blood would come out when you hit the ground that hard.

But if I get Mother and it didn't happen, and I really, really, *really* hope it didn't happen, then that'll be bad too. Mother will look at me like I'm crazy, or get mad at me for *even imagining such a thing*, or will tell me, again, that I've been going to sleep too late since Father has been gone. Then she'll make me go to sleep early, which would be the worst, because even if it didn't happen, I already have a feeling I'm not going to be able to fall asleep tonight for a long, long time.

I stand there not knowing what to do, but soon that doesn't matter. Because I see it. Them, actually. Out of the corner of my eye. The couple. Facedown, still holding hands, their bodies in the shape of a crooked V, which is barely five feet away from the marching soldiers. Who barely seem to notice. I don't see any blood, but that doesn't make me feel any better, not at all.

I take a few slow steps to the window and call out, "Mother," but the word doesn't make much sound. Dozens and dozens of soldiers are marching right past them, like that crooked V is nothing more than some sheets someone left outside by mistake. I try calling Mother again, but my throat won't work.

What kind of army trains you not to notice people falling out of the sky? What kind of soldier marches perfectly straight even when he's marching right past a crooked, dead V?

And that couple, did they know something the rest of us don't? Is there a chance they weren't just crazy? Like, I don't know, maybe they were in Germany a couple of weeks ago and saw what it's going to be like here. Maybe they were barely able to escape from Germany and thought they'd be safe here. Maybe they're not crazy at all, because they know there's nothing worse than living where the Nazis are in charge.

I know it's not nice to think this, but I sure hope they were just crazy. Even if that means being crazy enough to jump like they did. Because if they weren't crazy, if they knew exactly what they were doing, well, then I don't even know what that means.

Suddenly I feel like going to my room too. I grab another cookie, but I have a feeling I won't eat it. Mother walks out of the bathroom when I reach the hallway. My mouth opens to tell her what I just saw, but then it decides not to say anything. Maybe it thinks that if I don't say anything, it still might turn out to be something my eyes made up.

Mother leans over to kiss my head, but I make sure not to slow down. I hear her say something about me practicing my violin, but I ignore it. Next thing I know I'm sitting on my bed, staring at a star-shaped cookie, one of its points broken off, the whole thing ruined by all that sweat in my hand.

October 2, 1939

"MISHA," FATHER SAYS ONE AFTERNOON after school, "how would you like to pay a visit to King of Railroads?"

I don't even answer. Just hop up and grab my jacket. Because King of Railroads is the best store in all of Prague. And I haven't been there in forever, since even before Father went to London, where he was for a bunch of months before finally coming back a few weeks ago.

While we're waiting for the elevator (our building was one of the first in the whole city to get one), I almost say, *I don't think we've ever gone to King of Railroads during the week.* But I don't, because maybe he'd change his mind then. So I just look at him and smile. And he smiles back, but I'm not sure he really means it. Or maybe it's just how tired he looks, even though if you saw him from far away you'd think he was the same as always, with his fancy suit and tie.

* * *

I rush out of our building before him and turn left, because ever since I saw that couple jump, I avoid the place they landed. Only he points with his thumb in the other direction and says, "Let's take Simackova for a change."

I feel myself start to make a face, but I stop it before he notices. Because I know why he said that. Because Veletrzni is off limits to Jews now. Because they won't stop making up new rules and regulations. The stupid Germans. And almost all of them are just for us Jews. We can't eat in most restaurants or swim in public pools or even go to German-language schools anymore (Marietta had to switch to a Czech one, but I was in a Czech one all along). They made us give up our radios, and starting about a month ago we're not allowed to be out past eight p.m. And it's not like I would usually be out that late, but still, it's not fair at all.

We even had to let Leci go, because people who aren't Jews can't work for Jews anymore. Her last day was the worst. She arrived extra early and cleaned and cooked like her life depended on it. Mother kept telling her to stop, kept telling her there's no need, kept trying to get her to come to the living room for tea. And when she finally agreed, Leci called out to me. So I went over, and she pulled me up on her lap like she used to years ago, even though I'm too big to be sitting on someone's lap. But I let her, because I could tell she really, really wanted me to. She just hugged me tight. Then she started crying, which made my mom cry. And me too, almost. So I slid off and went to my room.

Father and I walk past the spot. Where the couple landed. A day after that happened, I went down there to look, but I couldn't find any sign on the sidewalk. They didn't crack it or anything. And so I finally asked Mother about it, but she just shook her head and asked, *Why don't we talk about it another time?* Only that other time never came. I brought it up again once or twice, but I could see how just mentioning it made Mother really sad, so I stopped.

And honestly, it isn't that hard to forget about them jumping most of the time, because so many other horrible things keep happening. Like the million rules the Nazis keep forcing on us. A bunch are about money and businesses and banks and courts and things like that. When Father got back, I asked him to explain those to me, and he tried, but they still didn't really make sense. All I know is that we have a lot less money than before, because of what we eat (or don't eat) these days. Also, I don't think anyone in our family, including Mother, has bought a single new thing since the Germans invaded.

At first, even though the new situation was bad, I figured it wasn't going to last long, so it wasn't that bad. But now it is starting to last long, plus it gets a little worse every day, every time they make up some new rule, tell us some new thing we can't have, some new place we can't go. We can't go to most restaurants, we can't share a hospital room with a non-Jew. None of it makes any sense. Though maybe to that couple it did. Or would have, I guess. Maybe somehow they knew exactly what was going to happen here.

Plus, of course, there's actually a war going on now. Because Hitler wasn't satisfied with Czechoslovakia. He wanted Poland, too. Oh, and it's not even Czechoslovakia anymore. Now we're called the Protectorate of Bohemia and Moravia. Like we need their protection.

We turn onto Janovskeho, and I see Christina walking toward us. Her hair is so pretty today it's almost glowing. Maybe she did something to it since the last time I saw her, which now that I think about it was months ago. I wonder if it will feel different too.

I raise my hand to wave hello, but Father pulls it down right away. Christina sees us anyway. But then she looks away quickly and crosses to the other side of the street. She doesn't even say hi or wave. She just pretends she didn't see us in the first place, even though I know she did.

I turn to Father to ask him why she did that, but the sad, tired look on his face tells me not to bother.

"Misha," Father says when we reach the river.

"Yes?"

"I'm sure you've noticed that I haven't been working much since I got back."

I watch a boat glide under the Stefanikuv Bridge. It moves so slowly it barely makes any waves. Then I realize Father isn't saying anything. I turn away from the river and see him straightening out his tie.

"Yeah, I noticed," I say. "Of course I noticed."

"Well," he says, not moving his head. "I won't be . . . for the time being I won't be working at all."

His voice is very soft when he says this, not like his regular voice. With the cars passing on one side and the river making its regular watery river noise on the other, I barely hear him. I want to ask him to say it again, just to make sure, but something tells me that's not such a great idea.

"Oh," I say. He takes my hand, and I let him. We walk for a while without talking.

Then I realize something. "Does that mean, Father, can we go on outings during the week now?"

"Perhaps," he says.

"Hikes?"

"Possibly."

"Because, well," I say, my voice speeding up, "Lukas, a boy in my class, he says he has twelve badges on his walking stick. Including one from the Krkonosh Mountains. I don't believe him, but he won't bring it to school. He says his parents won't let him. Anyway, I only have eight. Eight? No, I have nine. Anyway . . . but so I thought . . . maybe we could . . . now that you have more time . . . maybe we could do a bunch of hikes. Stechoviche and Lovos and even—"

"We'll see, Misha, we'll see."

As soon as we turn the last corner, I race ahead and run inside King of Railroads. Right away the sound of all those model trains churning around and around the tracks pours into my ears. I rush up to the edge of the giant display. And there they are: a long, black steam engine pulling car after car of coal, and a sleek, silver locomotive with a half dozen red passenger cars behind it, and another train loaded with lumber and who knows what else inside its green cattle cars.

The trains snake around hills and past miniature forests and over bridges and through canyons. When they enter cities, white crossing arms automatically lower at every street. They travel so fast I'm always sure they'll tip over at the curves, but somehow they never do.

The door opens and soon Father is standing next to me. Neither of us says a word for a while. I should have started collecting parts for my own railroad last year. Now, because of his work, or because of his no work, and because they'll probably announce soon that Jews can't have model trains, I bet it will be hard to get everything I need.

"Can we take a real train soon?" I ask him.

"Perhaps, Misha," he says, placing his hand on my shoulder.

"The faster the better," I say. "I don't care where we go."

And then I try to remember: Are there rules against Jews going on trains? There are so many regulations at this point, I can't keep them straight anymore. And I'm pretty sure my parents can't either. They bicker more than ever, their voices always just low enough for me not to hear. They whisper like that all the time, even when they should be sleeping. I know, because sometimes, at night, I get up to go to the bathroom. And lately, every time, I see a light on under their door. It must be because of all these rules.

So I don't ask Father whether we can still go on trains. I decide we can. Because if the Germans don't like us so much, then of course they'd want to let us on trains. That way we could go somewhere else.

September 16, 1940

"HURRY, MISHA," MOTHER SAYS TO ME. "It is already three thirty."

"One more minute," I say. "I'm almost finished." With my homework, that is. Even though it's not real homework, because there's no real school anymore. Not for Jews, anyway. At the end of the summer they said we couldn't even attend Czech schools anymore. So now I go to third grade in the living room of Erik Laub's family. There are six of us there. Two older girls, who are supposed to be in college, teach us everything. We sit on wooden chairs in a circle and play cards instead of going out for recess.

"Misha," Mother says, suddenly standing in my doorway, not happy at all. "If we don't hurry, we won't make it in time."

To the store, she means, because now Jews are only allowed to shop from three to five each afternoon.

"Okay, okay, I'm coming."

"And you didn't practice your violin, did you?"

"So?"

"So when we get back, first thing, do you hear me?"

The tram comes and we step into the back car, even though the front car is way less crowded. Because that's another rule: Jews can only ride in the back now. There's nowhere to sit, so we stand while the tram rattles down the street. Mother says hello to a friend, but then falls silent and stares out the window over my shoulder.

She looks tired. She used to dress so fancy, but now she's in a plain gray dress. And no jewelry either. Over the last few months, she's been going through everything in our apartment, separating anything valuable. Anything valuable the Germans didn't take already, because they said we can't have cameras, typewriters, wool coats, or a bunch of other things. Including ski boots, because I guess the Germans don't want us Jews ruining their precious mountains. Which aren't even theirs in the first place.

And the valuable things she finds—paintings, jewelry, and her best dresses—slowly they've been disappearing from our apartment. She's been leaving some of it with non-Jews we know here, non-Jews who still talk to us.

The rest she sends to some warehouse in London. Our apartment feels so empty these days.

"When this is over," I say. "Will we get everything back?"

"What?" she asks, like I woke her from a trance.

"Nothing," I say, deciding not to repeat my question, or ask her the question that really confuses me: Why is no one willing to help us, or any of the other Jews around here, even though if things were the other way around, we'd help them?

At least I sure hope we would.

The tram comes to a stop and we get off.

"Forget it," I say.

The store, like the streetcar, is packed with people. With Jews. There are so many things I want—chicken liver, herring, salami, honey, fresh bread—but I keep quiet, because I know we can barely afford anything now. Father hasn't worked for almost a year, and even I can tell our savings are pretty much gone. So Mother takes her time, stopping every few steps to study the price of some item very closely. After what seems like an hour, she'll finally place something in our basket, only to remove it a second later.

We leave the store with just one bag and begin walking

back to where the tram dropped us off. But then Mother says, "Let's walk home instead."

And the walk isn't so bad, except when we pass a park with that stupid sign, JUDEN VERBOTEN, "Jews Not Allowed." A bunch of boys my age are kicking a ball around. Lucky.

"Misha," Mother says a few blocks later.

"Yeah?"

"I want you to know that . . ."

"Huh?"

"We will be moving soon."

"What?"

"From our apartment."

"Moving?" I say, like I've never heard the word before. "Why are we moving?"

"Our apartment is too big, and the—"

"No it's not. It's not too big at all. Our apartment is exactly the right size. What's too big about it?"

Mother doesn't say anything for a minute. We stand at a corner, waiting for some cars to pass.

"The Germans are ordering all the Jews to move into the old part of the city. By the Old-New Synagogue. Everyone will be living there. We'll start moving at the end of the week."

I find a stone on the sidewalk and begin kicking it ahead

of me. I bet I'm much better at soccer than those boys. But if I kicked the stone to them, to let them know that I play soccer too, they'd probably just throw it back at me. Like those other kids did last week, when I was on my way back from the Laubs' apartment. They even started chasing me, but I found a good hiding place near this one church and they disappeared. I still haven't told anyone about that.

"Will there," I ask Mother, "will there be an elevator in our new place?"

"No, Misha. The building we'll be in is much too old for that."

This stone is starting to hurt my toes. I kick it hard toward an imaginary goal, which I miss for some reason.

"And what about school?" I ask, right as we pass the spot where the couple landed. At least I won't have to think about them so much once we're gone. Even if what they did makes more sense every day.

"We'll find a new place for that as well."

"You mean a new apartment," I say, but Mother doesn't answer.

We turn onto our street, which soon won't be our street.

"Mother?"

"What?"

"If all the Jews are going to be there, in the old part, do you think they'll let us play in the parks there?"

"I don't know, Misha, we'll—"

"Just because I don't get to go to regular school doesn't mean I should get bad at soccer, too. Right?"

We enter our building, which soon won't be our building.

"Once we move there, Mother, and we're all there together, do you think they'll leave us alone?"

Mother doesn't say anything. The elevator arrives. We step inside and I press the number four, because Mother knows I'm in charge of the elevator. When we first moved here, I would ride it for hours just for fun. But now it doesn't seem so fun.

"Will they?" I ask again.

"We'll see, we'll see."

"What do you mean, we'll see?" I say, raising my voice. "All we see is that every day is worse than the day before. Every day is a new, stupid rule and worse food and no soccer and no one seems to care or want to help even though—"

"I know, Misha, I know," Mother says, getting out of the elevator.

And I realize I should probably shut up, but for some reason I can't. I pretty much yell down the hallway, "You said Father was going to figure something out. But he hasn't figured anything out yet, has he? Well, I think if he's going to figure something out, he should start soon. Because what if it gets too late? What if . . . what if they make up a new rule that makes his plan impossible? Then what?"

My voice echoes off the sides of the hallway, but Mother doesn't answer, she just lets herself into our apartment, which pretty soon won't be ours.

May 25, 1941

A MAN STOPS TO LIGHT A CIGARETTE IN the middle of the Old Town Square. Maybe he'll be interested.

"Excuse me, mister. Would you like to buy a belt?"

The man stops for a moment. "A belt you say?" Good, he speaks Czech. Whenever I hear a German accent, I put my head down and just walk away. And if I see a German soldier, well, then it's around the first corner as fast as I can make it.

"Yes, mister, a belt. Look." I hold up my latest work, a rope belt, my best one yet. "I braided it myself."

The man places his cigarette in his mouth and reaches out for the belt. Tugs on it with his fingers. He wouldn't wear it himself, I can tell, not with a suit like his. But maybe for his children, if he has any.

While he tests the belt, I scan the square for potential

customers. It's a Sunday, so there's plenty of families out. If I can sell one more belt, I might get to two hundred crowns. Enough to buy us some butter.

"And what do you charge for a belt like this?" he asks me slowly, as if I'm standing behind the counter in my very own belt shop.

I show him my friendliest smile. "Fifty crowns."

"Fifty?" he asks, his eyes narrowing. "That's pretty steep."

"Forty," I offer. But he doesn't say anything, just picks some tobacco off the edge of his mouth. I reach into my pocket and pull out another belt. "Two for sixty. It's a very good deal, mister."

"Sorry." He hands the first belt back to me. "Maybe next time, kid." Darn, and I was so close.

The man walks off leisurely, his hands clasped behind his back. Just before he disappears into a crowd, I see one hand reach up toward his head. He tosses his cigarette down to the ground.

Okay, hurry.

I rush over and pick up the cigarette from where it came to a stop, between two cobblestones. Excellent, there's at least a third still left. With the other stubs I've collected, I could probably roll up a good cigarette, maybe even two. I sold one last week for twenty-five crowns.

I feel around in my pocket. About 160 crowns. Oh well, better than nothing.

Clang, clang clang clang!

The old astronomical clock. I didn't even realize I was standing right under the thing. The massive tower is over five hundred years old, with dials that can tell you everything. The time, the day, the zodiac sign, the location of the sun and moon—you name it. Father once explained to me how all the parts work together, but I could barely pay attention because I was too busy watching the clock.

Clang clang, clang!

A strange skeleton up next to the clock does this every sixty minutes. Clanging in the new hour with a bell in his bony hand. And right above him, other figures, the apostles I think, pass by the windows that open whenever he clangs his bell.

Clang clang, clang clang clang!

They say that the man who built this, some clock master named Hanus, was blinded after completing this clock. On purpose they blinded him. That way he wouldn't be able to build another like it. I never used to believe that story. Because people can't be *that* mean, can they?

But these days, I don't know. Maybe they can. Maybe that's nothing. Because the rules just keep coming. We can't buy apples, we can't play the lottery, we can't ride in taxis, we can't go into hotels. Nothing's too small for them, nothing's too weird. Who cares if we buy apples—how could that possibly matter? And even though I bet a lot of Czechs hate the Nazis as much as we do, some seem pretty okay with this whole setup, the cruel signs in their store windows bigger than they have to be, JUDEN VERBOTEN, their new swastika flags flying out front first thing every morning.

Last week we turned in my violin, because that's another rule. Jews can't have musical instruments. The rule says we have until December to comply, but we gave my violin in early. Probably because I was so awful at it. I used to take lessons from my uncle Ota, and no matter how hard I tried, I never made a sound that didn't make both of us squirm. If I didn't know better, I would have thought my violin was meant for torture. Handing it to Mother was the first and only time I was almost happy about one of those new Nazi decrees.

Because overall I'm not happy. Not at all. Yesterday, when I was supposed to be doing my pointless homework, I suddenly was trying to figure out something the Nazis wouldn't do, some rule I couldn't picture them making. But I couldn't come up with anything. No food that would have to stay legal for us to buy. No place that would have to be okay for us to go. No item that they wouldn't tell us to turn in. All under the threat of "severe punishment" if we don't follow the new rules. Severe punishment meaning death, I think.

All of which means that this could actually get much, much worse.

Wait, how did it get to be six o'clock already? Mother will kill me if I don't get home soon.

Even though home isn't really home anymore.

I race through the narrow streets of the ghetto toward Kozi Square, where our apartment is. Our new apartment. That isn't new at all.

"Misha!" Mother says when she sees me. "Where were you?"

"Look, Mother." I show her my coins. "Almost two hundred."

"Big deal," Marietta says from the corner of the living room, a room that is also the kitchen and the dining room. She's sitting on her bed, her nose in some book as usual. My bed is in another corner, not too far from hers. Mother and Father sleep in the only bedroom. I bet three apartments this size could fit into our old one in Holesovice. Still, maybe I shouldn't complain. Plenty of other families, including in this building, have to share an apartment with other families.

"It's more than you made," I say, putting my belts and

loose tobacco in a small cigar box I keep by my bed. "Hey, where's Father?"

"At a meeting," Mother says, stirring something into what must be soup, because that's all we ever eat these days. I'm starving, but it will be horrible, I'm sure. Because you can't buy anything with the lousy ration cards the Germans give us. No apples, no oranges, no onions, no garlic, no cheese, no chicken, no fish, no anything. Most food you'd actually want to eat you have to buy on the black market, where everything costs way more than it should.

"What meeting?" I ask.

"A meeting," she says, not even bothering to look at me.

I was right, dinner was awful. And Father wasn't even home for it. Plus no one would play cards with me after. As soon as he did get home, he and Mother ran off to their room and closed the door. They only came out to tell me to get into bed.

I'm really hungry, if only I could fall asleep already. But I'm still not used to this place.

"Marietta," I whisper.

"What do you want?"

"What do you think Father is doing when he's gone so late?"

"What do you think? Trying to get us out of here."

"Do you think he will?"

"He better," she says. "He should have never come back from London. He should have done whatever he had to then to move all of us there."

"But so where would we go now? Now that he's back. I mean, the Germans are everywhere. And we don't even—"

"Misha," she says, almost nicely, "not now, okay? I just want to sleep."

The funny thing is that this apartment is only three blocks from the Old-New Synagogue. And we still go there, Father and I, even if we don't get to do our walk along the river anymore.

Last week we got to the synagogue early, and Father pointed at some metal rungs climbing up the pale side of the old building. About twenty rungs, the line of them curving just a bit as they go up, leading to the dark brown bricks right below the pointy, triangular roof. But then, for some reason, the rungs end right by a small door that's always, always closed. I mean the thing doesn't even have a doorknob.

"Do you see those, Misha?" he asked.

"Yes."

"They lead to the attic, right?"

"Yes."

"And do you know what's up there?"

"What?"

"Well, about four hundred years ago, there was a very great rabbi, Rabbi Loew. And he wanted to protect the Jews. So he made a creature out of clay that he gathered from the banks of the river."

"Our river?"

"Yes, of course. From the Vltava. And then he brought it to life. Using only the powers of Hebrew, Rabbi Loew gave it life. He put the name of God on—"

"The name of God? What does that mean?"

"Good question, Misha," he said, patting me on the shoulder. "I don't know. But *he* did. So he wrote it on a piece of parchment and placed the parchment in the creature's mouth. And just like that it came to life. A powerful creature. The Golem."

"Did it work?" I asked. "Did the Golem really protect us?"

"It did, it did," Father said, nodding his head. "Until the Golem grew too strong. And instead of merely protecting us, it started harming people who didn't deserve it. Even Rabbi Loew couldn't control him."

"So what happened?"

"Well, the rabbi tricked the Golem into coming close to him. He did it right here in fact, right where we're standing now. And then he reached—"

"How did he trick him?"

"You know what, Misha?" Father laughed. "I have no idea. But Rabbi Loew was very smart. So, somehow, he reached his hand into the Golem's mouth and removed the parchment."

"And that stopped the Golem?"

"Yes, it fell into pieces instantly."

I looked at the sidewalk, trying to picture giant lumps of clay everywhere. But it was impossible. "So what does that have to do with those rungs?"

"Right, right, Misha. Of course. That's where Rabbi Loew put him. What was left of him anyway. All those lumps of clay. And many believe the Golem is still there."

And I was about to ask Father if he thought it was a true story, but just then Petr Weiss interrupted us, because even though Father doesn't work anymore, he's still a very important man. So people always want to speak with him.

I can hear Marietta breathing loudly now. Lucky her, she's asleep. So I try to match my breathing to hers, because sometimes that works.

So why don't we go up there and get the Golem?

Someone must still know the name of God, and even with everything the Germans took, I'm sure we could find some parchment somewhere. And then all we'd have to do is put it back inside the clay mouth, and the Golem would take care of everything else. Just like that, no more Nazis.

Of course it might get out of control again and hurt people who don't deserve it.

But so what? Because what did we do to deserve this? What did any of us do? What did I do that made those kids want to throw rocks at me and chase me down an alley a few weeks ago? What did any of us do to make the Nazis threaten to kill us, just for walking into a hotel?

And if this all doesn't end soon, then what? What will worse actually be like?

It's no use; I can't fall asleep. I get out of bed quietly and walk toward their bedroom.

Amazing. Their light is actually off. I carefully open the door. Even more amazing, they might actually be asleep.

I lift myself up onto their bed, crawl toward their pillows, and squeeze in between my parents.

"Misha?" Father asks, half asleep.

"I couldn't fall asleep."

Mother mumbles something while Father lifts up the blanket and waits for me to get comfortable. Back in our old apartment, they'd never let me do something like this. And I wouldn't have wanted to anyway. But here it's okay.

Father drapes an arm over me and pulls me into his side, my ear pressing up against his pajamas. Somehow his breath reminds me of just how tired I am.

Maybe having the Golem again would help, but Father's pretty tough too. Plus he's probably as smart as that rabbi was. Or almost, which is still very smart. I bet he's going to come up with a great plan soon. Yeah, as long as Father's around we'll be fine.

September 8, 1941

THEY'RE NOT SO GOOD. IF I WAS ALLOWED in the park, I'd show them. I mean, that boy with the vest, he can't dribble at all. Still, it's almost fun to watch. Because later, when I'm in bed, it'll help me imagine a game where I can play. And in those games, I'm always the star.

Always a star. Exactly.

Because now there's always one on my chest. There has to be. That's the latest rule. A week ago Mother came home with a stack of stars. Yellow, six points. That makes it a Jewish star, a Star of David. At least that's what Father says. And in the middle, in thick black German letters, *Jude.*

Jew.

I should get out of here. If they see me peeking out from this doorway, they'll know. Now that I have a star, everyone knows. And if they know, they might come after me like the other times.

But that was a pretty nice goal, the boy with the big ears faked out the short one completely.

We spent the evening sewing the stars onto all our jackets and heavy shirts. Right over the heart. That's what Mother said when she gave me the needle and thread and let me try. But I was no good at it.

And so now, whenever I go out, I can't pretend anymore.

My hand's up there again. I keep touching it; I don't know why. Maybe I'm touching the star to cover it up, so I can pretend a little more. Or maybe just to make sure it's there. Because if you're not wearing one and they find out, it's like the thousands of other rules they've made—like the one from just a couple of days ago that says we can't use libraries or even go into one—you really don't want to get caught breaking one. But maybe I'm just not used to it. Because how are you supposed to get used to something like this?

One of the boys looks over, the biggest one. I really should go, because a few times already some boys have chased after me once they figured out I was Jewish. I didn't have a star any of those times, but that didn't matter, because why else would a kid stand at the edge of a park?

But the biggest boy, he smiles. Maybe he doesn't mind. Maybe he likes having a spectator. Maybe he wishes he could invite me to join them. Maybe he hates the Nazis as much as I do. He taps the one in the vest on the shoulder. Points my way.

"Hey, kid!" he shouts.

"Yeah?"

Suddenly there's a rock coming at me. One of the other boys must have thrown it. Just like last time, and the times before that. The thing lands a few feet in front of me and skips across the cobblestone.

Time to get out of here. I spin around and head in the other direction, half walking, half running. Zigzagging from doorway to doorway, stealing looks back toward the park. My heart beating hard against the star.

I turn down an alley and peek back their way. Good, no sign of them. My heart isn't convinced, but that's okay. After all, I got away from the same kind of kids those other times, why wouldn't I be able to now?

Maybe I'll head over to the square. Even though most people won't come near me now that I have this star, some folks feel bad for us and agree to an extra-high price. On Tuesday a woman led me into an alley just like this and gave me one hundred crowns for two cigarettes. It was amazing; I ran home to—

"So what do we have here?"

Darn, it's them.

"I told you, Oskar," the one with the big ears says, and before I can get a good look at his horrible smile, I'm off. Tearing down the alley. Another stone hits the ground and bounces past me. Then, ow, something nails me in the back, right below my shoulder blade. Probably a rock. Really hurts. The pain makes me want to stop, especially since it gets worse every time I lift my right leg, but I know I can't stop. Their footsteps echo off the walls. Or maybe those are mine. Or maybe it's just my heart.

Another alley. Quick, turn left. I almost look back to see if I've lost them, but not this time. Past a church, another right. If this is where the grocery store is, then that means I'm almost home. I try to listen for their steps, but mine are too loud.

Wait, where's the grocery store? Did I take two rights or a right and a left? And now which way? Why are my legs so tired? I used to be able to run for hours, no problem.

Okay, left. No, right. Then find a doorway and hide.

Oh no. Dead end. Darn. But maybe I lost them already. Because even though I can't run like I used to, I'm still way faster than most kids my age. They probably gave up.

Just crouch behind this gate and count to one hundred. They'll be long gone by then.

One, two, three, four, five, six . . . I'm definitely going to have a bruise where that rock hit me, and if Mother sees, she's going to forbid me from going outside at all . . . seven, eight, nine, ten, eleven . . . I swear, at this point, I'd rather be anywhere but Prague . . . twelve, thirteen, fourteen, fifteen . . . it used to be the best place in the world, but now, well now I'd take my chances somewhere else . . . sixteen, seventeen, eighteen—

No, it can't be. How did they—

"Over here!" the littlest one yells. "I got him!"

"Yes!" the one with the ears shouts. He's smiling again. The worst smile I've ever seen.

All four of them seem way bigger than they did two minutes ago.

"Please," I try, but then can't figure out anything else to say. My heart starts up again. This time not as fast, but much harder, like it's hoping to break through my ribs so it can go find another boy to live inside of.

"Please what, Jew?" the biggest one says, standing right in the middle of the only way out, his arms crossed.

I count to three again, jump up, and push past him, my shoulder colliding with his. I can see he's surprised, and maybe even impressed. But the other three are still there.

And now all four of them have their hands on me.

"Cut it out!" I shout. "Put me down!"

I'm twisting and turning and kicking my legs, but it's no use. They're too strong, and their laughing tells me they know it. The big one, who's got my left leg, reaches into my pocket. Pulls out three of my rope belts.

"Stop it! Those are mine!"

"Shut up, *Jude*," he says calmly, like I'm just annoying him. "Over there, Tomas," he says, and points with the hand holding my belts. "That'll do."

My back slams into a tree. The bark cutting right through my jacket and into my skin. But now my feet are free, so I take a quick step between the little one and the kid with the vest. They're the weakest and my best chance to escape.

Only the big one just grabs me from behind and throws me extra hard back into the tree. My head knocks against the trunk.

"Jew," he says. "Have I hit you yet?"

"No."

"Exactly. But if you try something smart like that again, I will. And then you'll realize it's a bad idea for a Jew to get too smart."

I say nothing, just look at each one of them. Maybe the one with the vest—I think that's Tomas—maybe he feels bad for me.

"Hey, Oskar," he says, "toss me those belts. I'll show you that knot I was telling you about."

The four of them stand together, about ten feet from me, admiring their work. I don't even bother tugging at the ropes anymore. That knot Tomas tied, it might as well be a padlock.

I stare down at the ground and tell my tears to stay inside, where they belong.

I figure they must be getting ready to leave, when suddenly Big Ears is right in front of me again. That smile is back, the one that crawls up only half his face. He tilts his head a bit, takes a half step back, grabs my pants, and yanks at them.

"Hey!" I yell. "What are—"

Only they don't go down all at once. Because of my belt. But that doesn't stop him for long. He reaches into his pocket and pulls out a tiny little penknife, the blade barely an inch long. And even though I'm struggling the best I can, he has no problem cutting through my pathetic belt. And then it's back to my pants. He yanks extra hard this time. My button goes flying, and just like that my pants are at my ankles.

My pants *and* my underwear.

"If his star doesn't convince someone"—Oskar points and laughs—"that sure will."

They run off, finally.

And now the tears don't care where they belong.

A long time later a man walking by unties me. He doesn't ask me what happened, and I don't bother telling him. I thank him without even looking in his direction.

I walk straight home, holding my pants up with my left hand, trying to figure out what I'll tell Mother about the button. Because I couldn't find it anywhere. Not that I searched for all that long.

October 14, 1941

"BUT WHY CAN'T IT GO THREE AND THEN one?" I ask.

"Because, Misha, those are the rules," Father says. "The knight is only allowed to move two spaces and then one more. Or one and then two."

"Chess has too many rules. I'm sick of rules. Why can't we just play Chinese checkers?"

Father looks over at Mother, who's sitting on the armchair, sewing up holes in our socks. We used to just buy new ones. We used to just do a lot of things. Like walk along the river, but even that's not allowed anymore. The best place in Prague, and they took that away too.

Somehow she senses Father looking at her, and her eyes lift up from the blue sock she's working on. She shrugs her shoulders.

"Misha." Father turns back to me at the kitchen table

where we're sitting. "I tell you what, ten more minutes of chess and then we'll play whatever game you'd like. How does that sound?"

"It's too complicated," I say, picking up one of my pawns and trying to stack it on top of another. Of course it falls, taking out a few more pieces in the process.

"You're right," he answers, putting my pieces back in order. "It's a very, very difficult game. But it is a beautiful game as well. And it will teach you to think, and that is—"

I try to listen to what he's saying, I really do, but for some reason I can't. And I was so happy this morning, when I got him to agree to be home by four o'clock to play with me. That's been the only good thing about all the changes around here. More time with Father. I was sure we'd play cards, or something I'm good at. But lately he always wants to play chess. Only it's so hard.

"And why," I interrupt him, "why if the king is the most important piece, why can it only move one space? I mean, what kind of king can barely move better than a pawn?"

Father picks up his queen. "How about this?" He places it off to the side. "I play without my queen." If Marietta were home, maybe together we could convince him to play marriage, the best card game ever.

I turn to Mother for help, but all she says is, "Misha, do you know what kind of soccer player Andrej Puc—"

"Antonin," I correct her, shaking my head and rolling my eyes.

Father gets up and walks to the sink, probably to see if he can get any more tea to come out of the bag he's been using for two days now.

"Do you know what kind of soccer player *Antonin* Puc was when he started playing?"

"Huh?"

"A truly rotten one."

Father laughs.

"Very funny. So?" I ask.

They've been ganging up on me like this a lot lately. "Misha," Father says, returning to the table. "When I began studying law, I was completely overwhelmed. I couldn't keep anything straight. And I was about to give up when—"

Two quick knocks at the door. Father stops talking. Mother stops sewing. I look back and forth between them, but neither of their faces will tell me anything.

"Should I get it?" I ask.

Two more knocks, louder this time.

Father places his mug on the table, walks to the door, and opens it. Two German officers fill up the doorway. Without asking, they step inside.

"Karl Gruenbaum?" the older of the two asks.

They're enormous. Father barely comes up to the chin of either one. They wear identical, dark gray uniforms and shiny black boots that almost reach their knees. Each has a black iron cross on his chest, and the tips of their collars are decorated with two different patches. Each has a patch with two straight-lined S's on it, or maybe they're two lighting bolts.

SS officers. What are they doing here? And how can we get them to leave? For a moment my throat closes up, and I can't breathe. I try to swallow, but carefully, so they won't notice.

"Yes, sir. That's me," Father says, nodding his head slightly. I feel myself trying to do the same thing, but my head won't move. And my effort to swallow only half worked, so I need to cough, but I don't, deciding to hold my breath instead.

The one who spoke has another patch on his collar, with three small squares in a diagonal line on it, almost like you see on dice. The other one, younger and even bigger, has a patch with only one square in the middle. Their hats have some kind of eagle or something near the top, and below that what I'm pretty sure is a skull.

Without moving his head, the younger one steadily passes his eyes over our whole apartment. When they get to me, they don't stop at all. Like I'm just a piece of furniture or something.

I decide to straighten out my pieces, even though they're already in order. I try exhaling through my nose, and it actually works. Thankfully, I don't need to cough anymore either.

"Come with us," the first officer says.

I wait for Father to say something, to ask a question, to talk his way out of this. He's the smartest person in the world, and these Nazis, well, they're big, but they don't look too bright. Why doesn't he invite them to sit down? Mother and I could take a walk and leave them alone so they can talk here.

But Father doesn't say anything, just walks to the closet and gets his jacket. After he puts it on, he fixes his plain white collar and tightens his tie. He looks at Mother the entire time, but neither says a word. After he finishes with his tie, he does nothing for a few seconds. Nothing at all. Just stands there, almost smiling. Meanwhile, the SS officers seem like they're growing by the second. And those are definitely skulls on their hats.

I turn my head to Mother. She's holding the needle and thread in midair, her hands not moving at all.

I'm about to say I'll play chess with Father for as long as he wants, but he speaks first.

"Ready."

The three of them turn around and walk out. Father closes the door behind them. I listen to their footsteps going down the stairs. Why didn't I hear them on the way up?

Then it's quiet.

"Well," Mother says after a few long seconds, "I can finish this later. How about . . . how about some Chinese checkers?"

"Where's Father going?" I ask.

"I'm not sure," she answers. "But I'm sure . . ." Mother walks over to the sink and gets herself some water. After she finishes drinking, she still stands there for a little while longer, her back to me the whole time. "I'm sure," she says, and walks over to me, "he'll tell us all about it once he gets back."

"Is he in trouble?"

Mother combs her fingers through my hair, even though she knows I don't like it.

"Is he?"

"Now why would Father be in trouble?" she asks, and walks to the closet, which is still open. She disappears inside it for a while, which is weird because I know she knows exactly where we keep the Chinese checkers. Plus there's not all that much stuff in there to begin with.

Eventually she comes out with the box in her hands. "So?" She smiles. "What color would you like to be?"

I'm about to say blue when I notice the queen, stranded at the edge of the table. It might be the strongest piece, but suddenly it seems so helpless over there, with nothing but a mug of weak tea to keep it company.

November 27, 1941

I KNOCK FOR THE THIRD TIME, HARDLY surprised no one's heard me yet. Because even out here in the stairwell the crying and babbling is too loud for me. So I try the doorknob, and it turns. I push the door open, and the noise bursts out all around me. I peek my head inside. There's Mother, with two tiny children in diapers on her lap. One is crying, and the other looks like he's getting ready to join in.

"Hi," I say.

"Misha?" She's confused. "That door shouldn't be unlocked. Hurry, come in, come in."

"Am I too late for lunch?"

"No, no," she says, placing one of the children on the floor and getting up to give me a hug. She locks the door. "But you'll have to help."

My mother's dress is spotted with . . . with I don't know what. White blotches, plus something orange or yellow. And her hair is sticking out everywhere. She always used to look like she was on her way to the opera. Now she works in a nursery and is wearing the same old dress she wore yesterday. But we need the money, and that was even before Father disappeared.

Father. We haven't heard anything about him for a couple of weeks. I don't even ask anymore, except when I can't help it. Which is about twice a day, at least. All we know for sure, he was arrested. Those Nazis didn't just want to "talk" to him. They arrested him and thirteen of the men he worked with before the Germans showed up. They took them all to the Pankrac Prison here in Prague. And now, every evening, until curfew, some of their wives come to our apartment, where they drink tea and whisper among themselves, the bags under their eyes a little bigger and a little darker than the day before.

Three boys, maybe two years old, grab my legs and giggle.

"Misha!" they scream.

"Will you keep them busy while I fix lunch?" Mother asks.

I herd them and two others about their size into the next room, which is really just the Kinskys' bedroom, even though you wouldn't know it with all the toys scattered everywhere. Because during the day the whole apartment transforms into a nursery. At least twenty infants and toddlers, with only a couple of women, Mother and Mrs. Kinsky, to take care of them. Marietta helps out sometimes too. I don't really help out myself, just leave "school" for a little while and show up for lunch, because whatever the children don't eat I get to finish off.

I try to convince them to build a tower with all these blocks, but they seem to think the wooden cubes are part of lunch. Meanwhile, a little girl has crawled into the room, her stinky diaper announcing her arrival.

I grab her below the armpits and carry her to the kitchen. I'm willing to play with these kids, but I wouldn't change a diaper this smelly for a royal feast. Actually, I would. But carrots and mashed potatoes are definitely not a royal feast.

The door to the kitchen is mostly closed, and I'm about to knock it open with one of my elbows when I hear Mrs. Kinsky, in the middle of saying something. ". . . transport order. The entire family. They're to report tomorrow."

"Transport." A new word we're suddenly hearing a lot these days. Because the Germans aren't satisfied with making up new rules every other day. Now they're going to make us move around, too. Like lumber on a train. It started last month, around the time Father was arrested. You get a pink summons, and then you have to report to the Exhibition Hall here in town. Next thing you know, you're off to Poland. Why, I have no idea. Part of me bets it's got to be better over there than here in lousy Prague, but who knows at this point.

"To Lodz?" Mother asks.

"No, Terezin," Mrs. Kinsky answers.

"Terezin?"

I peek through the crack in the doorway. They've stopped preparing lunch. Mrs. Kinsky wipes her thick hands on a small towel hanging off her shoulder. Even though there's not much food in the ghetto, Mrs. Kinsky still looks like she eats way more than she should. "It's here in Czechoslovakia. Not so far from Prague. An old military fortress. Ada told me her cousin, Herman—I guess he's a cook of some sort—was sent there a few days ago. To help set up."

"Set up?" Mother asks. "Set up for what?"

"How should I know? Perhaps—" But the mouth attached to this dirty diaper lets out a cry, and a second later the door is all the way open. Conversation over.

"Mother," I say about a half hour later, back in the kitchen, where I'm helping to clean up. Which in my case means wiping all the plates clean with my finger.

"Yes?" Mother's at the sink, washing the plates.

"What are these transports about? Why don't they want us in Prague?" She doesn't answer. "Mother?"

"I don't know, Misha," she says, scrubbing a bit faster.

"Do you think we're all going to wind up on a transport at some point?"

No answer.

"And now that they're sending people somewhere close, instead of Poland, is that better? Or worse?"

Nothing.

"Hey, maybe Father is there already." I swallow the last piece of carrot from the last plate. "Maybe they needed lawyers to set it up and not just cooks. Maybe that's why they took all the men he used to work with. Right? To help with the money or something."

Mother turns off the water. Wipes a spot above her eyes with her forearm.

"And if we do have to go there, we'll come back here once this is all over, right? When the war is over, I mean. If the Germans lose, that is. Which they better. Which they will, right?"

Mother comes over to me and moves some hair behind my right ear. "Misha," she finally says, "it's time for you to go back to your lessons. I'll see you in a few hours."

And just like that, she kisses me on the cheek, turns around, and leaves the kitchen to help Mrs. Kinsky, because even though the children are supposed to nap after lunch, at least half of them have other ideas.

December 18, 1941

MARIETTA AND I ARE SITTING ON OUR BEDS, her drawing and me reading the sports section of a week-old newspaper I found in a garbage can. But I can't concentrate, because this thing about Terezin is real. Aunt Louise and Uncle Ota left on a transport just a few days ago. And it's not like we used to see them all that much, but still, it's weird knowing they're gone, and to some place I don't really know anything about. Plus there's something about them leaving with Father still gone that makes the whole thing worse.

The door to the apartment opens. I'm about to say something to Mother, who I figure is the one opening the door, when I notice a weird expression on Marietta's face. I turn around, and for some reason Mrs. Kinsky is where Mother should be. She's even holding Mother's keys in her hand.

"Hello, children," Mrs. Kinsky says, standing there in her giant gray dress.

"Hi," we both say, a little confused.

She's holding a small box in her other hand. "I thought . . . ," she starts saying, but then stops.

"Where's Mother?" Marietta asks.

"She'll be here soon," Mrs. Kinsky says. After smiling for no reason I can think of, she sits down at the table and slowly opens the box. "I made . . ." Marietta stops drawing and makes a face, the one she makes when something is confusing or stupid, or both. "Would you like some cookies, children?"

A second later I'm next to the table, looking inside the box. How long has it been since I had a cookie, let alone *cookies*? They don't look like anything special. No chocolate, no powdered sugar, but they're definitely cookies, which is more than enough for me.

"Thanks!" I say, with one already in my mouth, and another waiting in my hand.

Soon Marietta's standing next to me, examining the box. For some reason she doesn't take one. Instead she lifts her head up, turns it to Mrs. Kinsky, and asks again, "Where's Mother?"

"Where's Mother?" Marietta says for the third time.

"Want one?" I ask Marietta, my mouth full of the second cookie.

"She needed to . . . ," Mrs. Kinsky says. "There was

something . . . something happened at the nursery, and she had to stay behind. Please, have a cookie, Marietta, they're delicious."

"They are," I say, already working on my third.

But Marietta just puts her hands on her hips. "What do you mean, *something happened?*"

Mrs. Kinsky makes a big smile and says, "Oh, Marietta, you shouldn't . . ." But then the smile disappears all at once, and her eyes open extra wide, looking sort of glassy. "Excuse me," she says, and hurries toward the bathroom. Before she even gets there, Marietta is out the front door.

A few minutes and a few cookies later, Mrs. Kinsky comes out of the bathroom. Her face and double chin are covered in splotches.

"Where's Marietta?" she asks.

"I don't know." My stomach does something. Something that hurts a little. "She left."

Mrs. Kinsky closes her eyes and exhales loudly. "Come, Misha, let's go." She takes my hand and, for some reason, kisses the top of my head. She smells like soap.

I can hear the two of them before we even make it to the nursery's kitchen. Both of them are definitely crying.

Mother raises her head when I walk in. Her face looks really pale and really red at the same time. My stomach sort of lurches, and for a second I'm mad at Mrs. Kinsky for bringing all those cookies. But then I realize something that makes my skin tighten up, all over my body, until everything hurts, until I can barely stand. I try asking the question, but all I can do is show Mother that I'm trying to ask it, and her eyes tell me she knows.

While Marietta sobs into Mother's lap, I try to get the words to come out. I think Mother is trying to smile to encourage me to say them. But it's too hard.

"Is he?" I manage to say a few seconds later. Mother nods, and then I'm not standing anymore.

I don't know how much time passes or how I wound up facedown on the tiling near the window, but Mother's next to me, rubbing my back. We stay like that for a long time, until my legs get tired of kicking the floor, and the part of me that is trying to make the rest of me die finally gives up.

"How?" I ask Mother, not lifting up my face. "How did it happen? How did he . . . ?" I'm crying, but the tears don't feel like mine. My whole face, my head, my whole body, none of it feels like mine. Mother doesn't answer, so I go back to kicking the floor.

I look up a while later. Mother's sitting on a thin wooden chair in the middle of the room. Her nostrils are open wide, and she keeps pressing her lips together. "The report said uremia."

"Uremia?" Marietta asks. She's sitting on the floor, not that far from me, her back against a cabinet, her head in between her knees. Her face so wet it shines.

"It's a type of kidney failure," Mrs. Kinsky says quietly.

"Father had problems with his kidneys?" I ask, trying to sit up.

"No," Mother says. "No, he didn't."

December 19, 1941

MOTHER IS HOLDING MY HAND SO TIGHT it hurts, but I don't say a word. I wonder if she's doing the same thing to Marietta with her other hand. At least I get a break sometimes, since she lets go of mine every minute or so to wipe the tears off her face. I keep waiting for mine to come again, but other than when I first found out, nothing.

The rest of the tram is empty except for the three of us, a couple of uncles, and an aunt. We're far from the ghetto. I'd ask how far Olsansky Cemetery is, but I know I should keep quiet.

The tram stops. "Come," Mother says. We get off. Eight of us. It's cold, so we stand close together. Cars pass by. So do people. A couple of them notice our stars, but they don't seem to care. Across the street, in big letters over the big gate, OLSANSKY CEMETERY.

We cross the street and walk through the gate. This

place is so much bigger than the cramped Jewish cemetery by the Old-New Synagogue, the one the Jews had to use for centuries a long time ago. That one got so cramped they had to stack the graves on top of each other. This cemetery, I can't even see the end of it.

I don't know who started first, but now Mother and Marietta are crying loudly. Marietta buries her face in Mother's chest. My uncle Arnost comes over to me and puts his hands on my shoulders. For a moment I hate him for being alive instead of Father, but when he pulls me into his side I just let myself fall against him. I close my eyes, and everything spins slowly while he rubs my back and says, "There, there."

A bit later we're all walking again.

We walk for what feels like forever, turning off the main paved walkway and onto a thin dirt path. There must be a million people buried here. The graves are all different. Some big, some small. Some are just wide, flat stones, some are statues of angels or Jesus. There are even these little . . . I don't know what they are, but they look like houses. And bare trees everywhere, getting ready for winter.

If Father were here, he'd tell me all sorts of facts about the place. I'm sure of it.

My face feels heavy. Or maybe just cold. No one talks. Up ahead I see a cart and two men. One of them is Rabbi Landau. A long wooden box sticks out from the back of the cart.

Father.

Uncle Arnost approaches the coffin, and his hand reaches out for the lid.

"Don't," one of Father's cousins says. Uncle Arnost doesn't say anything, just turns his head to the cousin. "There were instructions . . . not to open."

Uncle Arnost puts both hands on the edge of the wooden lid and raises it. His eyes close almost immediately, and he drops the lid back down, wood smacking against wood. Then he closes his eyes extra tight and brings his chin to his chest. Afterward, he takes a half dozen steps away from the group, his back to us.

When he turns around a minute later, wiping at the edge of his mouth with a handkerchief, he mumbles to the ground, "No one else can look. No one."

We're just a small circle. Standing around a deep hole. Rabbi Landau holds a small, old book in his hand and mutters in Hebrew. Next to him there's a shovel sticking out of a big mound of dirt.

We're Jewish and Father was killed for being Jewish and now we're putting him in the ground the way you do for a Jewish person. It doesn't make any sense.

My stomach hurts. Like it did all last night. From the cookies, or just from knowing.

Rabbi Landau gets to the Kaddish and everyone joins in. They do this prayer every week, so we all know it. Father used to say each word so clearly when I stood next to him in the synagogue, which the Nazis closed around the time they took him away.

But it doesn't matter, because I won't go back there again. I won't. Ever.

He told me it's a prayer for the dead. But all it talks about is God. Something else that makes no sense.

Rabbi Landau, Uncle Arnost, and two of Father's cousins lower the wood coffin into the ground.

They say Father's inside, but maybe they're wrong. Maybe the Nazis told Uncle Arnost to play along, and that's why he said no one else should look inside. Even if his face looked way too sick for someone who's just playing along. But who knows, maybe it's not him. Maybe it's someone else. Maybe Uncle Arnost just saw some other dead person, someone he actually knew. Or maybe it's no one. Maybe it's a bunch of rocks and maybe they didn't take him from the Pankrac Prison to some other prison, some place in Terezin called the Small Fortress. Maybe they didn't take him there and kill him. Maybe he's waiting for us back at our apartment in Holesovice and maybe the Nazis were just pretending and all this, all of the last two years, every last bit of it, maybe it's all a trick meant to teach me something.

But Mother wouldn't cry like this just for a trick. She couldn't. And they wouldn't cut our clothes for a trick, especially when we don't have all that much to wear anymore. And Rabbi Landau wouldn't play along, wouldn't cut our clothes the way you're supposed to when you're a Jew and someone you're related to dies. And we definitely wouldn't leave the ghetto and have someone dig a hole in the ground and pay for a coffin when we don't have any money, all just for some horrible trick that only teaches you that things can always get worse, much worse, even once you're sure they couldn't possibly get even a little more worse.

People are taking turns shoveling dirt into the hole. Onto Father in his wooden box.

My turn comes, but I don't want to. Because that would mean it's not a trick and he's not coming back. It would mean that I think we should still do Jewish things, even though they kill us for being Jews. And it would mean that soon we'll be done putting the dirt in the hole, because after that we'll have to get back on the tram, step into the last car, and go back to the ghetto, where we'll sit around and eat bread that cost ten times what it should and try to remember what meat tastes like. And wait for the summons that tells us now it's our turn for the transport, the transport that will take us someplace better, or someplace worse, or someplace just like here, which would be the worst of all.

I take the shovel and push it back into the pile of dirt. I take it out and push it back in. Over and over, faster and faster. I can't really see anything at this point, but I can feel my bottom lip moving up and down and something coming fast out of my nose. I throw the shovel extra hard into the dirt and soon, somehow, I'm lying on the pile. Marietta calls my name, but I don't know what she wants and I don't care. The dirt is hard and cold, and Father never took me to the castle again. And we never went to Stechoviche or Lovos, and he was the nicest person in the world and was supposed to make everything better and you shouldn't put dirt on a person like this or do something to them that makes it so no one can look at them in their coffin.

Hands are on my arms and shoulders and hips, so I squirm to get them off me. Marietta calls my name again, only this time she's much closer. I twist and turn fast so no one can grab me, so I can keep them from putting the rest of this dirt on Father. Sounds come out of my mouth, but they're not words, so maybe they'll keep everyone away.

This works for a while until two strong arms reach around my waist and yank me back up. They squeeze me so tight I stop making my noises. They squeeze me until I finally give up.

One of the arms lets go and wipes my face with a cold, damp handkerchief that smells like Mother.

"It's time to go home, Misha," she says into my ear.

"Home?" I ask, like she's still trying to play that trick on me.

She pulls her head back and nods a few times, not bothering to wipe her face, which is somehow still making tears. "I know," she says. "I know." Then she takes my hand. "Come, it's time to go."

So we walk off and leave Father in his flimsy box, the one that is supposed to protect him from all that hard, cold dirt.

September 23, 1942

KRYSTOF KRAL. IF ANYONE ASKS, THAT'S MY name. I live on Albertov Street. Oh yeah, and my father, Dominik, he works in the theater. He's an actor. You've never heard of him, really? Well, I meet him over here after school. If his rehearsal is running late, he sends me to the movies.

So that's why I'm going to the movies right now.

And why I'm not wearing a star. Other than the fact that I'm Christian, of course. No, definitely not Jewish. What makes you think I'm Jewish? My name is Krystof. What kind of Jew names his son Krystof? Not Dominik Kral, that's for sure.

Yeah, he's really skinny. Just like me. I know, I know, but we're just naturally skinny.

I check my chest again. Nope, no threads left. And I'm pretty sure you can't tell anything was there. I was worried

there'd be a mark, from the sun or something. But nothing, luckily. Still, I rub some spit on it, just to be sure. I
can't believe I'm doing this.

Krystof Karl. Albertov Street.

When I found those ten crowns in the stairwell this
morning, I knew. I knew that if I sold a belt, I could go.
So I found a doorway and yanked the stupid thing off. But
then I wondered, do I throw it out or stuff it in my pocket?
Because if it's in my pocket, and I get stopped by some
Nazi, I can say, *Here it is. Some boys ripped it off. That's why
this edge is torn, see? They ripped it off really hard. I'm going
home right now to sew it back on, I promise.*

But if I put it in my pocket, then it might just fall out.
When I don't want it to. Like when I'm buying my ticket.
And then what would happen?

So I tossed it in the garbage. No, not tossed. Buried. I
buried it in the garbage, in case someone walked by right
after. So they wouldn't see the star, and then me. And
then start asking questions.

I shouldn't be going, I should turn back.

Look at all this. Just a regular day on Narodni Street. Trams
and cars and people sitting in cafés. You'd never know that
the ghetto—which isn't even that far from here—you'd
never know that the crowded ghetto isn't all that crowded

these days. There are probably more Jews in Terezin than in Prague at this point. Unless they're lying about that, too, and are sending us somewhere else instead.

For some reason they haven't given us our summons yet. Mother says that's good. I'm not so sure. Because what could be worse than here? What could be worse than a place with new rules every day? We can't use public telephones, we can't visit the castle, we can't buy fruit, we can't buy hats, we can't buy newspapers, we can't own pets, and if we had any money left in the banks, we couldn't even get to it.

That couple, the one that jumped from the balcony, how did they know what was going to happen?

Well, all I know, I can't stand being here anymore. No real school, no parks, no money, no good food, no anything.

And no Father.

Hey, maybe I'll go pass people on the Legion Bridge after. Haven't done that in a while. Not sure I've ever done it at all on the Legion Bridge. Huh, maybe I could even pass some German soldiers. That would show them.

Maybe later. After the movie. Why are you going to a movie? I don't know, but I am.

Oleg's Apartment. That's a good poster. Looks like it'll be a pretty funny movie. Look at his glasses. You can tell it's going to be funny. Wonder what it's about. Well, time to find out.

Okay, just make sure not to sound Jewish. Whatever that means. She can't know you're Jewish. Make it sound like this is normal, like it's no big deal that you're going to the movies today.

"One, please," I say, handing my twenty crowns to the little woman in the booth. Good, she doesn't even look at me. Just looks down her nose at the newspaper spread out in front of her. Takes my money and pushes a ticket back through the window.

"Movie starts in five minutes."

"Okay. Thank you."

Excellent, excellent. I made it.

Too bad I don't have any more money. What I'd give for a box of popcorn, or some candy. Even just a handful of black licorice.

Where should I sit? Normally I'd go all the way up to the front, but that's where other kids will be sitting, and kids sometimes talk, and maybe they'll talk to me, and then they'll know. Somehow they'll know. And then . . .

So I could sit in the back. But what kind of kid sits in the back of a movie theater? A kid who's trying to hide, that's who. Someone will figure it out. And then . . .

Okay, okay, so just sit in the middle. In the aisle, or

the center? Aisle's fine, Krystof, stop worrying. All sorts of people sit by the aisle. Kids, adults, it doesn't matter. Just sit down.

I wish it would start already. Once it gets dark, I'll be fine. Once they can't see me, I'll stop sweating so much. Once the lights go down and the movie starts, it's like you don't really exist. Because no one's allowed to bother you then.

But what if someone comes in late, and they want to sit in my row? Then they'll have to squeeze in past me. What if it's someone I know, Dr. Ambroz, our old dentist, or no, what if it's Leci? Even in the dark she'd recognize me for sure. What if she tries to squeeze by me and notices me and starts crying and wants a hug?

So you'd ask her not to tell anyone. She'd agree, but then you'd have to tell her about Father.

That would be really bad. That would almost be worse than getting caught. No, it wouldn't. If you get caught for going to a stupid movie . . .

Fine, don't sit by the aisle. Move in.

Six seats should be enough.

Finally. I never thought this thing would start.

Ugh, stupid German newsreel. It's impossible to get away from them. Something about Stalingrad, wherever that is. Who cares? Great, so you can conquer any city you want. Great, you have machine guns and hand grenades and tanks. All you're going to do is turn the place into rubble, so what's going to be so great about having Stalingrad?

At least they didn't bomb Prague. Why didn't they bomb Prague? Well, at least they didn't. Even if they ruined it in just about every other way you can imagine.

Am I supposed to clap? Is there a German spy in the theater somewhere, dressed like a regular businessman? Do they send a spy into each theater to see who claps and who doesn't after the newsreel?

Excuse me, young man, we'd like to talk to you. We noticed you didn't applaud after the newsreel about our offensive in Stalingrad. Are you an enemy of the Reich?

Fine, so if people start clapping, clap a little. But not too much. Just clap natural.

Krystof Kral? Albertov Street. Hmm. Our records don't show a Kral family on Albertov Street.

Good, it's over and no one clapped. Of course no one clapped. Why would people clap for a stupid newsreel anyway?

Finally, the movie. Better be funny. Not that I feel like laughing at this point.

Oleg *is* funny. Look how he walks. Like his pants don't fit or something. And he can't says his *R*'s at all. And he's so nervous about renting a new apartment. How he pushes his glasses up every five seconds.

But look how much he's sweating. Having to pretend that everything is fine.

Laughing feels weird.

Shh, Misha, stop laughing. You're laughing too hard. It's funny, but it's not *that* funny.

Okay, just remember to breathe.

And that you're Krystof. If someone asks.

Misha? Who's Misha? I'm Krystof.

Why would anyone ask?

Shh, just watch.

Okay, stop laughing, Misha.

I mean, Krystof, stop.

Stop!

But I can't.

Breathe, just breathe.

But it's not working. And now people are looking at you. They're going to know. And no one is going to believe your stupid Krystof story. You don't look anything like a Krystof.

Why are you still laughing? The scene's over. This part isn't funny at all. Stop laughing!

Stop!

Ow!

Krystof, why'd you pinch me?

Because you wouldn't stop laughing.

You didn't have to pinch me so hard. That really hurt.

Stop complaining. Did you want to get caught? Do you still want to get caught? Keep laughing like that and they'll know. Those Nazis, they know everything. They probably . . . they probably got Father to tell them all sorts of things about you. And he . . . he probably told them, even though he didn't want to, even though he held out for days, he probably told them how much you like movies. I bet they have a spy here, sitting right behind you.

What are you talking about? No, they don't.

Oh yeah, what makes you so certain? What makes you think you know anything about what they do and why? You want to know one thing you should be certain of? When they catch you, and they will, you're going to wish that all they did was pinch you. Leaving the ghetto. Taking off your star. Who cares if it was just for a movie? They won't, that's for sure. A rule is a rule. A law is a law. They killed Father, and you still don't even know why. It's not like he actually did anything wrong. And now you're playing games with them? Going to see a matinee? Are you stupid or something?

Shut up.

A pinch was too much for you? Really? Well, what about when they do this—

Ow!

When they take your finger and pull it back as far as it will go, and then they pull it a little more—

Stop it!

Or they make you stick your tongue out and bite down hard—

Ouch!!

Bite down extra hard, so hard the tip just about falls off. Try calling yourself Krystof then. But it won't matter. It won't matter what you do, they'll never forgive you. They never forgive anyone. You make one little mistake, that's all it takes with them, you're theirs forever. You're theirs until they're sick of you, sick of asking you questions you can't answer, sick of hurting you. And when that happens . . . well, you know what's next, don't you?

Leave me alone.

The second Gruenbaum funeral in a year. That's right. If you don't stop shaking like that, that spy sitting right behind you right now won't even wait until the end of the movie. . . .

Shut up.

Stop shaking and I'll shut up.

But I can't.

Stop.

I can't!

Stop shaking! Stop shaking, Misha, or you're dead.

I can't! I'm trying but I—

Too late, you're already—

How did I get outside? Why am I outside?

And out of breath.

And dripping sweat.

And without a star.

What in the world are you doing outside the ghetto without a star on? Are you crazy? What kind of idiot tears off his star and leaves the ghetto to go to the movies?

Krystof Kral, that's who. The dummy.

Mother would be furious if she found out. She'd never let you go outside again.

Okay, just start walking. Take a deep breath and just start walking straight home. And figure out your story, because she's going to want to know where you've been. And no more movies. No more Krystof either. You're Misha Gruenbaum and you live on Kozi Street in the Jewish ghetto, because you're a Jew, like the star says.

You idiot.

This isn't the movies. This is the real world.

Unfortunately.

November 17, 1942

"PLEASE GO TO SLEEP, MISHA," MOTHER SAYS.

"How long?" I ask.

"What?" she asks, exhausted and confused.

"How long until you'll be back?"

"Go to sleep," she says, picking up the suitcase. "I'll return soon."

The door closes behind her again. For what better be the second-to-last time. The last time will be when she comes back. Because Mother promised she wouldn't go out again after this one.

And she probably won't, because there's nothing left to take anymore. I walk back to the bedroom with my eyes closed, because I know the floor is completely empty except for our bags in one corner.

I try to get comfortable next to Marietta, but Mother's mattress just isn't big enough for the two of us. Mother took mine and Marietta's away yesterday. The day after the pink summons finally came for us. It wasn't the first time actually. A month ago was the first pink summons, but Mother got us off somehow, because of who Father was in the Jewish community I guess, because the committee that decides which Jews go when is actually made up of other Jews. But she couldn't do anything this time, because sooner or later your turn is going to come.

Tomorrow we go to Terezin.

She didn't seem too happy about it, but at this point, what do I care? We don't own almost anything anymore, and the rules just keep coming. Maybe it won't be better there, but I'll take my chances.

Margarete, Marietta, and Michael Gruenbaum. Summoned for November 18, 1942, at 8:00 a.m. to the Exhibition Hall in Holesovice for the purpose of deportation to Theresienstadt.

Theresienstadt. What the Nazis call Terezin.

Starting a month or two ago, I noticed things gradually disappearing from this apartment, even though we barely had anything here. Our fancy silverware. The rug that had been rolled up in the closet since we moved here, because it was too big for any of the rooms. The framed paintings that used to hang on the walls. And then the summons arrived and suddenly Mother went into high gear. Packing up just about everything that was left. Sheets, dress shoes, books, our dishes.

Not that there's any point in having dishes anyway. Not when there's almost nothing to eat. I haven't seen an egg in weeks. And I can't remember the last piece of meat I ate that was big enough that I had to actually chew it.

For over twenty-four hours now, Mother hasn't stopped moving. Out the door with a couple of suitcases packed with stuff. Then back home a few hours later with the suitcases empty.

Except when she came back this afternoon.

"Where are you taking everything?" I asked her when she slumped down into a chair with a glass of water.

And she mentioned some name. The name of some non-Jewish friend, a name I didn't recognize. Some old neighbor from Holesovice, I guess. She said the name, and then she opened up the suitcase and took out a couple of giant duffel bags. Told me to put anything I didn't plan to wear today or tomorrow inside one of them. Had Marietta do the same. Because you're not allowed to bring more than one hundred pounds of stuff per person.

But we're taking much less, because how is a twelve-year-old kid supposed to carry that much?

*   *   *

I listen closely for her footsteps, even though I know she won't be back for a while.

She better come back. Out past curfew, just to save a down blanket.

I listen closely for what seems like hours but hear almost nothing. Every once in a while the building creaks. Otherwise that's it. Which makes sense, since our building, totally packed with people when we first got here, is almost empty now. All our friends disappeared one by one. We must be some of the last Jews going to Terezin.

Eventually the door opens. Mother's steps grow louder. Just before she gets to the room, I try to roll closer to Marietta. Mother lifts up the thin blanket and joins us. Her body is cold and warm at the same time.

I almost tell her she didn't come back soon at all. But instead, I pretend I'm asleep. Because why make her worried that on top of everything else I'll be tired tomorrow?

November 18, 1942

THE TRAM STOPS AT VELETRZNI PALAC. I can't believe it, we're back in Holesovice. The three of us get off, along with a couple dozen other Jews. Their large bags and suitcases, along with the fact that they've dared to leave the ghetto in the first place, tell me they've been summoned too. As soon as I reach the sidewalk, I notice, up ahead, a long, long line of people, everyone carrying their things, just like us.

I'm marching between Marietta, who's in front of me, and Mother, who's behind me. Both of them are carrying large suitcases. I have a small bag strapped to my back and a much heavier one that I hold in my hands. I let myself switch hands whenever we stop. The canvas handle cuts into my palm, but it isn't too bad. Marietta's hair swings back and forth when she walks, so I try to concentrate on that.

I can't remember exactly how near we are to our old apartment, but I have a hunch we're pretty close.

People are heading off to work with their briefcases, trams are winding through the streets, kids are walking to school with bags on their shoulders that don't look all that different from mine. Of course their bags aren't packed full like mine is, because they still have homes where they can keep things they don't need right now. Every last thing I now own is in one of my two bags.

Wherever we are exactly, it's some totally regular section of Holesovice. Or at least it was regular Holesovice until our parade arrived. Because the second people see us, they stop whatever they're doing—getting out of a car, riding a bike, leaving a store—and stare at us. A few hundred tired, starving Jews dragging themselves down the sidewalk. Some people turn away, some wipe their faces like they don't believe it, some might be crying. A few kids, probably friends with those jerks who tied me up to that tree, point and laugh.

We reach a major intersection. The signs say Veletrzni and Belskeho. Of course, I knew it. We're only a few blocks from our old apartment. If we turned right here, we'd be there in less than five minutes. But instead of doing that, we keep marching straight ahead.

We pass Babka's. I look through the window at the

high tables. In a few hours, when it's lunchtime, all sorts of lucky people will stand there and gobble up delicious frankfurters, the grease flowing right into the soft rolls every time they take a bite. We pass Belskeho Bakery, where Mother would buy that wonderfully fresh rye bread filled with caraway seeds. The best bread in the world—what I wouldn't do for a slice right now. And the tailor's shop where Father took his suits and Martin's apartment and the pharmacy and that weird building with the bright red door.

We're almost at Simackova Street when I see someone standing under an awning on the other side of Belskeho. Someone familiar. A woman. A woman so familiar I can't think straight for a few seconds. Before my brain tells me her name, I notice all the parts of her I know so well. Her wiry hair, her long face, her thin fingers, her beaded handbag, her brown jacket with the pink flowers sewn into the collar.

Leci.

I see her before she recognizes the three of us, even though she's already frozen, her mouth a little red dot, staring at our pathetic parade. I tap Marietta on the shoulder. "Look! Leci, she's over there. Look!"

Then she sees us, and her eyes open wide. I sort of half wave to her with the hand holding my bag. And for a second, I'm almost happy, like she's somehow going to cross the street and pull out a plate of cookies or ask me what I learned in school or even wipe something off my chin with the edge of her apron. But then she begins to cry, and not just a little. I swear, in a single moment she goes from nothing to her face being half-soaked, the black from the makeup around her eyes running down her cheeks.

"Go, Misha, go," Mother says. I start to march again, telling myself not to look back.

A minute later, I see it up ahead: the massive Prague fairgrounds, the Exhibition Hall somewhere inside it.

"Anyone caught hiding valuables," the SS guard with the huge shoulders standing at the edge of the tables says loudly, "money, jewelry, et cetera—will be shot." His long, thin face says this like he's just an usher announcing the time for the next show. The Exhibition Hall is filled with the kind of noise a few hundred people make automatically, but each time he says this—which is about every ten minutes—everyone quiets down completely. His voice echoes for a second or two, and then the buzz starts up again.

"Mother," I whisper the third time he says it, and pull her head down to my mouth. "Don't hide anything, okay?"

Without looking at me she says, "There's nothing left to hide, Misha."

"Promise?" I ask.

She kisses the top of my head but doesn't say anything.

For some reason I breathe in extra hard, and this weird, gross smell hits me. I can't figure out what it is exactly, but it makes me think of the time I went to pee in a station at the very, very end of a tramline. Father and I were setting out on a hike. He told me, "Wait five minutes, Misha. Go in the forest." But I couldn't wait, so I hurried into the station's bathroom. The light inside the freezing, filthy room was flickering on and off, and the whole place reeked like it hadn't been cleaned in forever.

That's what it smells like here, only much, much worse.

There are about twenty people in front of us in line. In this line, that is. Because after you talk to the person at this table, you have to wait in line for the person at the next one. When someone finishes with one table, they take their stuff and drag it to the back of the next line. I'm tired, I'm hungry, and I'm bored. It's not fair that on top of everything else, we have to stand here like this. The least they could do is give us numbers or something and let us sit down until our number gets called. Then we could read or play cards or even just rest. But no, they want us to stand instead.

Finally we get to the front of our line. Sitting behind the table is a Jewish man with glasses resting at the end of his nose. Mother hands him our pink summons. He reads it, looks up over his glasses at the three of us, bites his thumbnail, and starts leafing through a giant stack of papers. It takes him a while, but eventually he crosses something out. Then he takes three small rectangles of mostly white paper from another corner of the table. The man, looking back at the summons Mother handed him, writes out one of our names on each piece of paper.

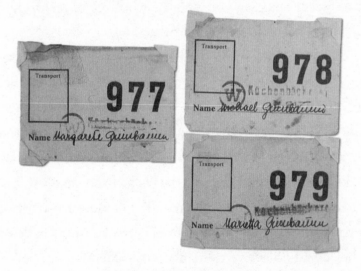

977, *Margarete Gruenbaum*

978, *Michael Gruenbaum*

979, *Marietta Gruenbaum*

He grabs a stamp, pushes it into an ink pad, and quickly stamps a *W* on each rectangle, right above the name. He extends all three rectangles to Mother.

"Thank you," I say.

The man doesn't answer me, just chews on his thumb again. Its bright pink skin is badly torn.

"What's that transport box for?" Marietta asks.

"It's for the name of the transport we're on." Mother says. "They must have left it blank because everyone here is on the same transport as us, Cc."

"Cc?" I ask. "Why Cc?"

"They started with A," Mother says. "Last year. After they got to Z, they started over at Aa."

I think for a few seconds. "So we're on the twenty-ninth transport?"

"Anyone caught hiding valuables," the SS guard says again, "money, jewelry, et cetera—will be shot."

At the next table another man with a yellow star on his chest asks us for our rations book. Mother gives it to him. The man, with curly hair and a big bald spot on the top of his head, flips through the book before tossing it into a cardboard box at his feet. The thing is half-filled with them.

"But how will we eat?" Marietta asks Mother in a loud whisper.

"You won't need those there where you're going," the man

says with about as much emotion as the SS guard. "Next."

When we're halfway to the next table, where people are handing over their keys, I tell Mother, "I need to go to the bathroom."

Mother scans the whole hall slowly. "Can you wait?" she asks.

"How long?"

Mother looks down this line, then over at the lines for the next two tables.

"Marietta," she says, "take Misha to the bathroom."

"But I don't have to go," Marietta says.

"Marietta," Mother says, "please."

"But what about our stuff?"

"I'll watch our things. Just please go."

"I don't even know where the bathrooms are," Marietta says.

"Then ask someone," Mother says, brushing something off Marietta's shoulders.

It takes us a while, but eventually we find a sign that says MEN'S LATRINE.

The smell is much, much stronger here.

"Hurry up," Marietta says, lifting her shirt collar up and over her nose.

I walk through an entranceway and then down a thin corridor, the smell growing with each step. The corridor turns and then opens up into a square about half the size of my old classroom. The stench makes something rise up in my throat. Against one wall is a row of metal buckets. Blue puddles surround each bucket.

A man with gray hair and pale legs squats over the bucket farthest from the entrance, his back to me and his pants down past his knees.

Marietta runs into an old friend on the way back to the tables. They hug and chat like they're in between lessons at their old school. I stand a few feet away and wonder how the Exhibition Hall can keep filling up with people. The line behind the first table is now a hundred people long, easy.

After the last table we take our bags and walk to the other end of the building, where rows and rows of small mattresses lie on the floor. People have already grabbed the ones closest to the rear wall, their bags piled up in the narrow spaces between the mattresses.

We reach the far edge of the unclaimed mattresses and throw our stuff down.

"Now what?" Marietta asks.

"Now we wait," Mother says.

"How long?" I ask.

"I'm not sure." Mother unbuttons her jacket, even though

the hall isn't very warm. "A day, two days. Maybe three."

I don't say anything, just plop down onto my mattress. The thing barely breaks my fall though, since it's really just a long, narrow sack filled with straw.

Someone peed on Mother's mattress not so long ago. We grab our things to move somewhere else when a Czech policeman, patrolling the room, tells us moving is strictly forbidden.

A couple of hours later they call us for lunch. We get in line and show our badges to someone who checks our numbers off from a long list and hands each of us a tin bowl.

I try counting while we wait. Around the time I get to five hundred, some man dumps half a potato and some nearly brown liquid into our bowls. I guess it's soup.

There's nothing to do here. Marietta disappears for a while after lunch, looking for that friend of hers. I see a couple of boys my age, but I don't know them. Plus there's nowhere to play here anyway. So I open my bag and take out the one book I packed. *Klapzubova Eleven.*

It's pretty much the best book ever, because the Klapzubova family is probably the best family ever, even if they're just made up. The Klapzubova family is the dad and his eleven sons. And they're eleven because that's how many people you need for a soccer team. Not only is every one of the brothers an amazing player, they all play separate positions. For a while they were worried, because none of them was any good in goal. But then the youngest brother, Andrej, he turned out to be a natural.

I've read it about ten times, but it never gets boring.

So I just open it to the place where they accept a challenge from the top club in Prague, which really wants to beat the Klapzubovas because the oldest brother, Lukas, who is probably the best player in the whole family, refused to sign with them. Of course he wins the game with a bicycle kick, his specialty.

And I'm nearly at the spot that describes him leaping up into the air with his back to the goal when I hear a loud thud, followed by a bunch of people up on their feet about ten mattresses from me. I put my book down and walk over. It takes me a while to see through the small crowd.

An old woman has collapsed.

Dinner is the same as lunch, plus half a carrot. Which I counted to 617 before getting.

I don't remember falling asleep, just thinking I never will. The giant hall is mostly dark, but it's never even close to quiet. Babies cry, sick people moan, and a thousand people toss and turn on their cruddy straw mattresses. At one point, in the middle of the night, I'm suddenly awake. I turn over and notice Mother. She's sitting straight up, her face frozen, her eyes open wide.

November 19, 1942

THERE IS ABSOLUTELY NOTHING TO DO HERE.
Except hold in my pee for as long as I can.

I count to 429 before getting breakfast, which is something I don't recognize. It's nearly white, very mushy, and tastes like paste. When we finish and return to our things, Mother removes a loaf of bread from her bag and lets me and Marietta split a quarter of it.

More people arrive, but not as many as yesterday.

A different, shorter SS guard threatens to shoot people hiding valuables.

An SS officer screams at the man working behind the table who kept biting his thumb yesterday. The man says something, and the Nazi slaps him hard on the back of his head twice. When I look over there an hour later, some-one else is manning that table.

I play a game with some boys in a corner of the hall. Using a crumpled up piece of paper, we play keep-away until some woman screams and makes us stop.

The Klapzubovas beat the Italian national team on penalty kicks, Andrej deflecting the Italian captain's try with the tip of his pinky. The ball hits the crossbar, bounces high up into the air, and falls back down, right into Andrej's arms. It was the first time ever the Italian captain had his shot blocked.

Lunch is the same as yesterday. But I had to count until 714 to get it.

A woman calls out Mother's name. It's the wife of one of Father's old coworkers. Holding hands, they talk for over an hour. Then they hug for a very, very long time.

Every once in a while I somehow forget that it smells like pee here. But at some point I always remember again.

* * *

The old woman who collapsed yesterday hasn't gotten up yet today. A woman around Mother's age spends pretty much the whole day sitting at her side and wiping her forehead with a damp cloth.

After I ask her about fifty times, Marietta finally agrees to play cards with me. But she doesn't try, and so I beat her easily, which is no fun.

Before dinner (a carrot and some broth with little pieces in it that might be chicken) I get up the courage to go to the bathroom. On the floor about twenty feet from the entrance is a young man with a very puffy face. He's sitting cross-legged in the middle of the bare floor. There's no mattress or bags near him. A badge with the number 741 is pinned to his chest. He's singing or moaning or both and keeps hanging his thick tongue out of his mouth while he rocks back and forth. As I pass him, I notice he's wet his pants. He rubs his hands back and forth in the puddle surrounding him. Then he sticks one of his hands into his pants, but not into his pocket. He sticks it in around the back actually. Something tells me I should look away, but I don't, or can't. He removes his hand a few seconds later, a clump of something dark brown stuck to the tips of his fingers. The next thing I know, he's eating it.

My stomach feels like it's about to turn inside out, so I

run into the bathroom, inhaling the stench there as much as I can. But even with my lungs full of the bathroom's horrid air, I'm not distracted nearly enough. Worse than that, something tells me that just like with the couple jumping a few years ago, I'm not ever going to be able to forget what I just saw.

I slowly walk toward our mattresses, my stomach still turning over and over and over on itself.

"I think I'm going to go to sleep," I tell Mother when I get back.

"So early?" she asks.

"Yeah," I say. "I'm tired."

She leans over to kiss me good night, and as she's sitting back up I grab her shoulder.

"Mother."

"Yes."

"Do you remember . . ."

"Remember what?"

"Nothing."

"What?"

"When I was much younger, you used to . . ."

"What is it, Misha?" I pull her even closer. "What?"

"You would . . . ," I whisper, "you would rub my back to help me fall asleep. Can you—"

"Of course, sweetie." She smiles a bit and closes her eyes. "Of course."

So she does, and if I concentrate hard on her hand as it glides back and forth along my skin, I can almost block out the sight of that man and the smell and the bickering and the moaning and the footsteps and the straw poking into my chest and that woman, ten mattresses away, who keeps begging, "Please, Mother, please. You must drink something. Please."

November 20, 1942

"UP! UP! EVERYONE UP!"

Czech policemen and a few SS guards are walking around screaming at us, even though it's still pitch-black out.

"What time is it?" Marietta asks.

"I don't know," Mother says. Of course she doesn't, she sent her watch to London almost a year ago. "Very early I think."

Maybe an hour later, after everyone has packed up and eaten a horrible breakfast, they have us standing in five long lines, according to our numbers. The black outside the windows is now pale gray. Everyone is holding all their things, or has them on the ground next to them. Regular German soldiers have arrived, a couple dozen of them, and they stand along our lines with bayonets in their hands. About twenty people ahead of me in line I see the old woman. Somehow she's actually standing. Well, not standing exactly, but she's upright and leaning on that other woman, her daughter.

After all the lines have been formed, an SS officer enters the hall. I don't think I've seen him before. He looks older than all the other soldiers and officers here. His face is pretty fat. The room knows to shut up the moment he clears his throat.

"Today you start a new life, in a land free from persecution. In Theresienstadt." His last word echoes in the hall for a few seconds. No one makes a sound. "There you will join thousands of other members of your race already living in perfect safety. Upon your arrival each of you will be assigned work, and in this way you will thus be given the opportunity to become productive members of the Reich. Your new future begins today. Heil Hitler!"

Even after the officer finishes speaking, turns quickly on the heels of his shiny boots, and leaves the hall, no one says a word. Maybe because everyone is stunned just like me. A new life? A land free from persecution? Safety?

Is there a chance he might actually not be lying?

"Mother," I whisper to her. "Do you think he's lying?"

I think Mother nods, but I'm not sure, because we've started marching forward.

* * *

I don't know how far they plan to have us march, but at this rate it's going to take forever. People seem to stop every ten steps to adjust their bags. At which point someone always bumps into the person in front of him. One time an older man trips over a large bag. A German soldier goes over to him, grabs him by the arm, and begins to lift him up. But then he just throws him back to the ground and kicks him in his side. The man doesn't get up.

The old woman and her daughter step out of our line. The daughter leans her mother against the side of a building. When a soldier walks over to them and points his bayonet at the mother, the younger woman puts her hands together like she's praying. Then we turn a corner, so I don't see what happens next.

The Praha-Bubny station. So that's where we're going. The station's plain gray building waits for us across Bubenska Street. Behind it a few long trains peek out, ready to take us to Terezin.

"Nine hundred to nine hundred and fifty, this car!" an SS guard shouts, and points. People begin to load slowly, stuffing themselves and their bags into the train. There are six or seven tracks here, and our train is on the second of them. Past the station there isn't much to see, except some small hills spotted with just a few buildings. At some point the clouds disappeared, so the sky is blue.

"Nine hundred fifty-one to one thousand, this car!" he says and points again.

A few minutes later I'm stepping up the stairs and onto the train. We stuff whichever bags will fit under our seats and leave the rest in the aisle. The three of us squeeze into a single bench.

Out through the window I see three people approach. The old woman and her daughter, plus another Jewish man. They're carrying her actually, it looks like she's asleep. Maybe she passed out again. Then they're in our car, and the sound of the daughter crying rises over all the other voices.

I lean my head against Mother's side. The sun warms my head. My eyes close, and I see the faces of boys pointing and laughing, their white teeth bouncing up and down. I see Leci, and the man sitting in that puddle, and my pants around my ankles, and the rungs leading to the Golem's attic, and that couple falling through the air, and Father putting on his jacket and never even saying goodbye to me.

I'm so tired that I can't pretend I'm not the saddest

kid in the world. And I'm so sad my empty stomach hurts and my face hurts too, like it's been crying for weeks, even though it hasn't. Then I realize I'm too tired to care about being so sad, so my sadness just sits there in my empty gut, like a thing that doesn't really have anything to do with me anymore.

But as the train jerks into motion, that feeling disappears, and in its place something else shows up, something unfamiliar, something I haven't felt in a long, long time.

Relief.

Good-bye, Prague.

Part II
Terezin

November 20, 1942

"MISHA, MISHA, GET UP. WE'RE HERE, GET up, get up." Mother is softly pushing my shoulder. I open my eyes. Marietta stands in front of me, putting her arms through the straps of her backpack.

"Where are we?"

"Bohusovice," Mother says. "The train station."

"Bohuso . . . ? But aren't we . . . ," I say, rubbing my eyes, "I thought we were going to Terezin."

Mother doesn't answer. She and Marietta are already heading toward the aisle, filled with people moving toward the exit.

I get off next to a building around the size of a very big house, its walls somewhere between faded yellow and faded orange. There aren't as many tracks here as there were back in Prague, and there's almost nothing beyond them. Just some mountains way off in the distance. The tracks themselves keep going, who knows where to.

The narrow platform overflows with people and their bags. Guards shout angry, impatient instructions. I follow Mother and Marietta around the building, where bags are being placed into a giant cart. A long line of people walks along the edge of the muddy street leading away from the station.

Right after handing our things to a young Jewish man in a cap, who tosses them up onto the cart right in front of us, I see the daughter of the old woman. She's sitting under a small tree maybe fifty feet from here, her arms wrapped around her legs, her head buried between her knees. I watch her for a few moments until someone tells me to move. I turn aside and see two men carrying something long, which is wrapped up in a couple of blankets. They place it carefully onto the very back of the cart, at the edge of the high mound all our things have made.

"C'mon, Misha," Marietta says. "Let's go."

So we join the line. Maybe ten minutes later the cart passes us. The back wheels pop up into the air for a second as the whole thing goes over a bump. It lands with a thud, and the end of the blanket falls open, showing me a pair of feet, their toes pointing down to the ground at two totally different angles.

*   *   *

Around a half hour later we turn off the main street and walk across a small bridge of sorts. On both sides below are fields with a small canal running down the middle. Up ahead a massive redbrick wall with gray cement stones running along its edges waits for us. The thing has to be twenty feet high. A big arched gateway has been cut out of the middle of it. Somehow there's grass growing above the top of the wall.

We reach the gateway and enter an arched passageway, probably a hundred feet long. Everyone's feet make strange, soft echoes inside it. For some reason no one says a word. When we reach the end of the passageway and find ourselves opposite a large, wide, almost-yellow building, I ask Mother, "Terezin?"

She closes her eyes and nods her head.

"How old are you?" a Jewish man, this one with a lot of stubble on his face, asks me. He's sitting on a low stool behind a wooden table that has a thick crack down the middle. The table and his low stool are the only furniture inside his windowless office, which we entered off the passageway itself, meaning the whole thing is inside the wall of the fortress. People, including kids, are walking in and out all the time. I have no idea why.

"Twelve," I say.

"Twelve?" he asks Mother, raising one of his bushy eyebrows.

"Yes," she says. "He's twelve. His birth date is August twenty-third, 1930."

The man doesn't respond, just opens a notebook to a page containing a chart with lots of numbers and what might be abbreviations. He studies the chart for a minute or so, tapping the tip of his pencil inside a few different boxes and humming to himself the whole time. Then he shakes his head and maybe laughs, too. "Pavel!" the man shouts.

A boy a few inches taller than me appears. "Yeah," he says, exposing a gap between his two front teeth.

"Take this imposing young man to L417, room—"

"Excuse me," Mother interrupts, shaking her head back and forth very quickly. "L-4-1-what?"

"L417," the man says slowly. "One of the buildings here, the Children's Home. For boys. He'll be in Room Seven. One of the boys' rooms."

"Children's Home? One of the what?" Mother asks, and then her mouth just sort of hangs open.

"What's a boys' room?" I ask Marietta.

"Pavel," the man says, "would you like to explain?"

Pavel scratches his arm. "Kids live with kids here, not with—"

"What do you mean?" Mother closes her mouth, but

her top lip keeps doing something really strange.

"I'm in Room Seven too," Pavel says, like it's all no big deal.

"But he . . . ," Mother starts saying. And I want to say something too, because suddenly my chest hurts really badly. But I keep quiet.

"Pavel," the man says, taking a deep breath and wiping his forehead with the back of his hand, "how often do you see your father?"

Pavel shrugs one of his shoulders. "I don't know. Pretty much every day. If I want. Depends."

"What about your mother?" I ask.

"Pretty much?" Mother asks.

"Yeah, pretty much," Pavel answers.

Mother is silent. There's a little tear in her right eye, but it's just sitting there. I look at Marietta, whose face suddenly looks kind of gray, like it was carved out of an old rock or something. My chest really hurts. For some reason I turn back to Mother and tell her, "It'll be okay, right?" So maybe I ask her. She hugs me so hard that the pain in my chest sort of breaks all apart, which feels horrible and good at the same time.

The next thing I know, I'm outside, following Pavel, who says "C'mon, hurry up" a few times, until he stops, turns around, and asks, "Hey, what's your name, anyway?"

*   *   *

We walk past one big, wide building after another, each separated by a small street. It kind of looks like we're just wandering around some small city.

"What is this place?" I ask Pavel.

"What do you mean?" he asks. "It's Terezin. What else would it be?"

"No, but, I mean . . ."

"The Nazis call it Theresienstadt. Whatever. Same thing."

We turn a corner. Instead of another building, we pass by a big square, with what sort of looks like a circus tent in the middle. At the far end of the square is an old church. Tons of people wearing stars are walking around all over the place. All ages, including lots and lots of old people. Even more are just sitting on benches or standing by the entrances to all these buildings. "I mean, did they build it just for us?"

"Nah," Pavel says. "It's been here for a while. Over a hundred years. Used to be an army fort, I guess. But now it's ours. Well, not exactly ours. It's the Nazis', obviously. But we run it. The Jews, I mean. Well, sort of, because mostly the Nazis just tell the Jews who run it what they have to do. But still, at least this way you barely ever have to see actual Nazis. Just Jews pretty much. And there's a lot of us here. Way too many, if you ask me."

We get to a pale yellow building with a brown roof. Pavel hops up a couple of stairs. "L417. C'mon."

It kind of sounds like a school inside, the way a school sounds when all the classroom doors are shut, but you can hear everyone making a racket, anyway. We go down a hallway and then up some stairs. Then down another hallway, until Pavel stops and opens a door.

A ton of noise spills out. "Room Seven," he says. I peek my head inside, but don't enter.

The room is probably the same size as a classroom. A small classroom. But instead of desks and chairs, there are bunk beds everywhere. Triple-decker bunk beds built out of plain wood, with wooden ladders leaning against each one. The bunks are all jammed together, so I can barely see even halfway to the back of the room. Plus there's all kinds of stuff hanging off the beds. Shirts, pants, jackets, shoes, blankets, bags—you name it.

And kids. Everywhere kids. All boys around my age. Lying on beds, sitting on beds, standing next to beds. Talking, drawing, writing, reading books, playing cards, setting up a chess board. A few more kids sit at these very narrow wooden desks set up between the rows of beds.

And a couple of boys might be wrestling on the floor below one of the desks.

"C'mon," Pavel says, grabbing the edge of my coat. "Don't just stand there."

I take about three steps inside. A few boys notice. "Hey, everyone!" Pavel screams. A few more kids look my way, but only a few. "This is Misha." No one seems to care too much. "So, okay. That's Kikina." He points at some kid with light brown hair. "And that's Shpulka"—though I can't figure out who he means—"and Pajik and Gorila—"

"Gorila?"

"And Majoshek and Extraburt and Robin and him, huh, him I don't remember, must be new, too, and I think that's Petr, and, oh, forget it."

"How many kids live in this room?"

Pavel takes off his jacket and tosses it on the top of one of the bunks. "About forty," he says. "About."

I try to get my mouth to say something to someone else, or my feet to move somewhere, but I'm sort of frozen.

"Hey," Pavel finally says to no one in particular. "Anybody seen Franta?"

Jirka keeps snoring. Well, not exactly snoring. It's more that every time he breathes in, he sort of gets stuck on something, in his nose I guess, right at the end of the breath.

Actually, I'm not so sure his name is really Jirka. It might just be Jiri. I met so many kids today, I can't keep any of their names straight. There was Paul and Martin, plus Erich, Jan, and Koko. And Hanus and Leo—there might be two Leos, maybe even three. There are definitely two Hanuses. And Mendel and Egon and Jila. And a bunch more I can't remember now. Well, whoever this kid is who's lying right next to me on our mattress, he keeps snoring.

I can't sleep. I guess I got used to how quiet the ghetto was by the time we left Prague. Somehow Marietta always slept like a rock back there. Where is she right now? And Mother? One of the boys, maybe it was Mendel, said that women sleep in some place called the Dresden Barracks, wherever that is, and that if Marietta is sixteen, she's considered a woman here. So I guess they're together. Lucky them.

But not me. Nope, I'm sharing a room with forty other boys I barely even know. And about half of them seem like they're having some really important conversation, even if it is in their sleep. One boy will murmur something, and a second later some other kid sort of answers him with a grunt. And they'll go back and forth for a while until someone else joins in. Then all three of them will argue, until one gives up, at which point the two left take it from there. It's been like that for the last hour at least.

And where's Franta? I'm pretty sure Kikina said that he has a bed in the corner over by Pavel's, but I don't think he's there.

Unlike everyone else, when Franta met me, he actually seemed to care.

"Misha," he said, and even shook my hand firmly. "Welcome to the *Nesharim*."

"Neshawhat?" I asked, still standing by the entrance to our room.

"Nesharim," some boy with wavy brown hair said, Kapr maybe. "It means 'eagles.' We're the eagles. And Franta's our *madrich*."

"Huh?" I asked.

"It's Hebrew," Kapr said.

"Yeah," a new kid, short like me, said. Maybe it was Leo. "'Nesharim' is Hebrew for 'eagles.'"

"No," I said, really confused. "The other word." I looked to Franta for some help, but he just stood there with a little smile on his face.

"What other word?" Kapr asked.

"The other one . . . that you said Franta is."

"Hey." Leo elbowed Kapr. "He means madrich."

"Right," Kapr said. "It means counselor. Or teacher, or guide, or something like that."

"In Hebrew," Leo added.

"Oh," I said. "Okay."

Franta nodded quickly and rubbed his large chin for a few seconds, looking down at us. He wasn't that tall for an adult, and not too old, either, like he almost could still be in high school. "Jila," he said, pointing to a third boy who had put down some cards and walked over to us. "What should Misha know about being part of the Nesharim?"

"Well," Jila, who has a lot of light brown freckles on his cheeks, said, "twice a day . . . twice a day you've got to show Franta you're clean. Hair, face, hands, nails. Stuff like that."

Franta lowered his eyebrows and nodded. His dark eyes darted over to me, which for some reason made me look away. It wasn't that his eyes were mean or scary, but I couldn't look at them when they were looking at me. At least not right then. "Good," he said, "what else?"

"You've got to make your bed," Kapr said. "Every morning."

Franta nodded seriously, but didn't say anything.

"And bedbugs," Leo said. "We check our beds for them every day."

"Plus for other insects," Jila added.

Franta nodded his head a few more times. "What about bathrooms?"

"We clean those, too," Kapr said.

"And," Leo said quickly, "if your hands and stuff aren't clean, you have to clean the toilets!"

"Which are really, *really* gross," Jila said, raised his shoulders, and squeezed his eyes shut.

"Is that all? Do we merely clean all day long here?" Franta asked.

"It feels that way sometimes," Leo said.

"Nah," Kapr said, "we have the Program a lot of the day."

"Program?" I asked.

"It's like classes," Jila said, "like school. Well, sort of anyway. They call it that because we're not allowed to have official school. But still, we have that in the morning and afternoon most days."

"Unless you have a job," Kapr says. "Then you're allowed to miss the Program."

And I was about to ask what he meant by a job, when I noticed Franta scanning the room slowly, rubbing his chin again. "Misha will sleep next to Jiri," he finally said. Or was it Jirka? "Jila, go show him where that is."

And I took a step to follow Jila, only then I felt a hand on my shoulder. I stopped and turned around. It was Franta's hand. His fingers were lean and strong, which I bet are how Andrej Klapzubova's fingers look. Franta squatted all the way down to my height and looked right at me. I wanted to turn away again, but this time I couldn't, even though it felt like his dark eyes, just by looking at me, might knock me over. He looked back and forth at both my eyes. Maybe he was trying to figure out something really important about me. Then he squeezed the muscle that runs between my shoulder and my neck. He squeezed it pretty hard, but it didn't really hurt. It sort of felt good actually, and for some reason made me stand up straighter.

"Misha," he said, like he was just trying out my name. Then he lowered his eyebrows. His eyebrows weren't that thick, but the skin below them was, which is maybe what made his eyes do whatever they were doing when he looked at me. "Misha." He said it again. Then he nodded, rubbed my back, and popped back up. "Welcome, Misha. Welcome to the Nesharim."

So that's what I am now, one of the Nesharim. And the only one who can't fall asleep.

November 23, 1942

"HEY, MISHA," FELIX SAYS.

I just finished lunch, if you can call it that. After I waited in line for twenty minutes (where I started to count numbers again, only to forget at around fifty each time), they gave me a hard roll, some awful soup, and a little bit of spinach. For the tenth time in the last ten minutes I check my pocket for my meal ticket, since Pavel said you definitely don't want to lose that.

"Yeah?"

"You like soccer?" he asks.

I nod my head. "Why?"

"C'mon," he says, and heads toward the barracks' exit.

"Wait," I shout. "Where are you going?"

"Where do you think?" he answers.

I try to catch up. "But I thought . . . aren't we supposed to . . . don't we have rest period now?"

We get outside, and Felix races over to Pedro, Brena, Koko, Erich, Pudlina, and Gida. Pedro's holding an actual soccer ball in his hands, but I've never seen such a dirty one in my whole life. I swear the dirt looks about five times dirtier than regular dirt. But who cares? It's definitely a soccer ball.

"Hey, I didn't know you played goalie," Felix says to Pedro. "I don't play goalie," Pedro answers, like Felix just accused him of being a girl.

Koko slaps the ball hard out of his hands and starts laughing, "So then why are you holding the ball with your hands?"

Koko starts dribbling it down the street, with the other kids right behind him, all shouting for him to pass. I open my mouth to ask my question again, to double-check that it's okay not to be in Room 7 during the rest period, which is where Franta told us to be, and to see if it's okay to be going wherever it is we're going instead. But then Pedro shouts, "Last one to the *bashta* is the odd man!" So I sprint to catch up.

Bashta? What's the bashta?

We reach the end of the street, cross over onto some grass, and then run up a small hill. Next thing I know, we're standing on top of the fortress's inner wall, which is covered in half-yellow grass and sort of looks like a small field. I guess this is the bashta. A few more kids I don't know are already waiting for us.

I barely beat Brena up here, which I can't believe, since I know I used to be way faster than I am now. But that's what you get living in the Prague Ghetto and eating small portions of pretend food for the last two years.

"Lucky for you, Brena," Felix says, and kicks the ball of dirt to him, "there's ten of us."

The kids start passing the ball around to each other, but I'm so winded I can barely stand up straight. I act like my shoes need retying. The truth is my shoes need reshoeing, but there's no way that's happening. The grass is still a little damp from the rain yesterday, and my knees get pretty wet when I kneel down.

Pedro and some other kid toss their jackets down by one end of the field and measure the distance between them by taking tiny steps where your toe touches your heel, which is how we used to make goals sometimes back in Prague. "Sixteen!" Pedro shouts toward the other end of the field, where Pudlina and Felix are doing the same thing. Then Felix and Gida walk off a bit from everyone and start whispering and pointing, including at me. Someone kicks the ball my way, and I try juggling it a few times on my knees, but I keep messing up, maybe because the ball could use some air. I give up and just kick it over to one of the kids I don't know.

And then I notice—how did I miss it before—that there's a pretty good view up here. Past the gardens and the outer walls, past the river, all the way to a bunch of other buildings, including some houses. They couldn't be more than a thousand feet from where we're standing. Do regular people live over there? Regular people who can just come and go whenever they feel like it? People who can do whatever they want, including not stand in long lines for tiny, lousy meals and not sleep in rooms crammed with forty other people, where you get only one little shelf for all your things, which actually turns out to be plenty of space, because you barely even own anything anymore?

And do they have any idea what's going on inside this place? That it's packed with more than fifty thousand people with yellow stars on their chests? Which has to be ten times more people than should be here to begin with? Fifty thousand prisoners who still don't know why they're here or what they did wrong? And that maybe kids and regular adults can somehow handle it, but for some reason the old people can't, because yesterday I saw a cart with at least ten of them, all dead, being pushed right down the middle of the street running right past our building. Most of them were covered in blankets, but only most. Like it was no big deal, like this is just—

"Misha! Misha!" Gida shouts, and elbows me.

"Huh?"

"Didn't you hear me calling you?"

"What? Yeah, of course—"

"So can you play wing or not?"

"Yeah," I say, because I can. At least I could, back when I used to play soccer, whenever that was.

"C'mon," Felix says, "One to zero. No problem. Time for an equalizer."

It's me, Felix, Brena, and two other kids against everyone else. Felix is amazing. I can't even tell if he's a righty or a lefty. And Brena might be slow, but he's a pretty solid goalie, because it could easily be 3–0. The other two kids—I think their names are Gustav and Arnosht—they aren't bad defenders, but when Pudlina has the ball, they've got no chance.

Which means I'm the problem. It's like my feet have never seen a soccer ball before. And I'm still out of breath. The other team keeps doubling Felix, leaving me open. Like right now. And here comes another pass my way. Only I can't do a thing with it. Gida just takes it from me again, like we agreed I'd give it to him all along. Plus my shoe keeps coming untied.

I look up from my stupid laces to see Gida score, again.

"Sorry," I tell Felix a couple of goals later. The last one made it 3–1. "I swear I used to be good, I swear."

Felix isn't looking at me, just biting the edge of his lip. "Don't worry about it." He wipes his sweaty forehead with his sleeve. "Just cut to the goal. I'll get it to you."

And I try, but I'm actually getting worse somehow. I ran to the goal, like he told me to, and he got it to me, like he said he would. But when I brought my foot forward, I somehow kicked the entirely wrong side of the ball, and the thing shot straight out of bounds.

I can tell Felix is fed up with me, because now he's trying to do it all by himself. But as good as he is, his brother Pudlina might even be better. Together with Pedro, they're too much for him.

"Goal!!!!" Pedro shouts.

4–1.

I'm about to offer to switch with Gustav and play defense when Brena comes over, grabs the edge of my sleeve and pulls me to Felix.

"I think I know what the problem is," he says to Felix, and I feel my face get heavy. I'm about to tell them I just remembered I promised to help Franta with something after lunch, when Brena adds, "He doesn't know the chant."

Felix squints at me. "You don't?"

Chant? What chant?

I shrug my shoulders.

"*Rim, rim, rim, tempo Nesharim,*" Brena says very quietly. "Gustav and Arnosht aren't Nesharim, so technically we shouldn't be using it right now."

"*Rim, rim, rim, tempo Nesharim?*" I ask.

"Yeah," Felix says, "Go, go, go, Nesharim. It's our chant. For when we play other rooms. Franta made it up. He's our coach."

"We have a coach?" I ask.

"Of course we have a coach," Felix says. "What kind of team doesn't have a coach?"

"We have a team?" I ask.

Brena laughs. "For sure we do. And we're good, too. Way better than Theresienstadt Sparta, that Gustav and Arnosht play on. A few weeks ago we killed them, six to one."

"Seven to one," Felix says.

"Can I be on the team?" I ask.

"Are you one of the Nesharim?" Felix asks

"Yeah."

"*Rim, rim, rim, tempo Nesharim,*" Brena says, nodding his head, almost singing.

I try it out. "*Rim, rim, rim, tempo Nesharim.*"

"*Rim, rim, rim, tempo Nesharim.*" Felix says it, and a

moment later we're all saying it together in a low, loud whisper, our heads nearly touching.

"C'mon!" Koko shouts from the other side of the field. "Enough of the chitchat."

Felix pats my shoulder a couple of times and pushes me over to my side of the field.

And it's not like my shoes are any better or my lungs suddenly remembered how to switch to high gear, but something's different. Every time I mess up, which is about every thirty seconds, I tell myself, *Rim, rim, rim, tempo Nesharim*, and it's like . . . well I don't know exactly what it's like, but it's good. Or at least not so bad.

Felix passes me the ball, and I actually control it this time. I think about shooting, but instead, just as Pedro's almost on me, I pass it back to Felix, who flies past Erich.

4–2.

Rim, rim, rim, tempo Nesharim. I tell it to myself over and over. The words match up with my breath and somehow bring it under control.

Gida's dribbling toward me, when I suddenly figure it out. He likes to fake right and go left. So, just like that, I put my foot out by his left. Next thing I know, I have the ball. I kick it over to Felix.

4–3.

Rim, rim, rim, tempo Nesharim. By now the words are

just repeating themselves in my head. I don't even have to think them. And the voice is mine and not mine at the same time. It's a bunch of voices actually. Felix's and Brena's for sure, but then there are other voices too.

Like Franta's. And I barely know his voice, but I hear it loud and clear, probably because this was his chant first. I hear how he explains stuff to us and reads us stories and tells us to get out of bed in the morning. The way his voice is always super firm and super kind at the very same time.

The ball's headed my way. *Rim, rim, rim, tempo Nesharim.* But those aren't the only voices. Because I hear Father's voice too. Of course I do. Because he's the one who would always tell me not to get upset when I made a mistake. He's the one who always said I could do whatever I wanted if I just focused. He's the one who picked me up after I fell off my bike the day he first taught me how to ride. He squatted down, hugged me, and wiped the cut on my knee. When he asked me, almost in a whisper, if I was ready to try again, I was. And five minutes later I could ride as if I always knew how.

It's so weird, because I realize I've been trying *not* to think of Father. For months now. Because why feel that sad all over again? But this time, thinking of him makes me feel something else, too. Sure I'm sad, but I'm more than that, I'm whatever the name is for not feeling that everything's always going to be as bad as it's been lately, for feeling that maybe this place, Terezin, might actually be kind of good overall.

I control the ball and look out over the field. Gida's in front of me. Pedro and Erich are over by Felix. If I can get past Gida, that leaves just me and Koko, their goalie.

So I decide to give Gida a little dose of his own medicine. Fake right, go left. And what do you know, now I'm dribbling fast toward Koko. He's bearing down, waiting for my shot. I plant my left foot and bring my right forward.

Rim, rim, rim, tempo Nesharim.

I kick the ball harder than I've ever kicked a ball before. But it just sort of makes a weird fart sound, bends around my foot, and squirts ahead a few feet. The voices in my head disappear, and soon I'm just standing there in the middle of all that silence, on top of the fortress wall, staring at a huge dent in the dirt.

"Oh, man!" Koko shakes his head and runs over.

Felix arrives, picks up the dead ball, and flattens the thing between his hands. The ball offers up one last fart.

"I told you that liner was about to go," Gida says, catching up to us.

"Sorry," I say, but no one says anything.

"I heard that Room Nine has a decent ball," Felix says.

"Or we could just play with the rag ball," Koko says, "like we did last week."

"No way," Gida says, "a tin can is better than that thing."

"No it's not!" Koko says.

"Whatever," Felix says. "We need to get back anyway. Tie game."

"Tie?" Koko says. "What are you talking about, tie? We won four to three."

"Misha was about to score," Felix says. "You saw it, he was—"

"*About* to score," Pudlina says, grabbing the flat, dirty circle and throwing it pointlessly back toward the rest of the camp.

The four of them, along with everyone else, run down the hill, kicking the flat ball back and forth and arguing about the score. I look back at the houses on the other side of the river, take a couple of deep breaths, and race to catch up.

November 26, 1942

"HEY," JIRI SAYS, "WANT TO HEAR A JOKE?"

"Sure," I say.

"Okay," Jiri says, leaning on his rake. "So, two Jewish kids are walking along a street in Prague, when two guys from the SS approach them. They stop the Jews and ask, 'Who started the war?' The Jewish kids answer just like they were taught to. 'The Jews,' they say. The SS soldiers are satisfied with the answer and start walking away from the boys. But then they hear the boys say something and laugh, so the Nazis come back and say, 'What did you say? Why are you laughing?' So one of the Jewish boys says, 'And the bicyclists.' The soldiers, very confused, ask, 'Why the bicyclists?' So the boy shrugs his shoulders and replies, 'I don't know. Why the Jews?'"

I smile, but don't really laugh.

"Don't you get it?" Jiri asks.

"I think I do," I say, and start laughing a little.

"Hey, Kapr," Jiri says, "Misha doesn't think the bicyclists joke is funny."

"Because it isn't," Kapr says without looking up from his rake.

"What are you talking about?" Jiri says. "It's hilarious."

"Hey, who's that?" I ask Jiri.

He drops his small rake to the ground and rubs his nose with the back of his hand. "Who's who?" he asks.

"That girl," I whisper, even though she's probably a hundred feet from us.

Jiri follows my eyes over to the line of girls our age spreading hay or straw over the dirt we've already raked. We're preparing the gardens for the winter, not that I know what that actually means. But somehow Mother got me this job out here, I guess she wanted me to be out in the fresh air. All the guys say this is a good job, even if I'm not exactly sure why. So I work here all day, instead of participating in the Program. I'm still not sure how serious that whole thing is, though I did hear one of the guys talking about a test yesterday.

What I do know for sure is that there aren't many plants left at this point, though every once in a while I notice a carrot in the dirt that someone missed. Every time I see one, it's like seeing a little bit of gold, because in just the short time I've been here I've already noticed we're getting less and less recognizable food to eat. And it's not that I like vegetables very much, but here you're glad to have anything that you know is real.

"Which girl?" Jiri asks, a little annoyed. "There's got to be thirty of them over there."

"That one." I point with my elbow. "With the red hair and the blue thing on her head."

Jiri softly kicks Kapr, who's still raking, on the heel of his boots. "Guess who finally noticed Inka," he tells him.

"Inka?" I ask.

Kapr looks over at me, shakes his head, but doesn't say anything.

"What?" I ask.

"Good luck" is all he says. No one says anything for a bit, so I just look at her some more. It's weird, because I don't really care all that much about girls. But I can't stop noticing her. Because it's not so much that she's pretty, even though she definitely is. It's that if somehow, instead of us getting in a line, marching up the ramp, and turning into the ghetto, we turned the other way and were suddenly back in Prague, she'd look like she belongs. After she took her star off, of course. She looks, I don't know, *normal*. It's like she reminds me how everything used to be. And maybe could be again.

"The worst part," Jiri says, "she's really nice, too."

"C'mon, you two," Kapr says, motioning with his head toward one of the guards at the edge of our group, "get back to work. I don't want to get in trouble."

Twenty minutes later I'm still watching Inka, when I see the strangest thing. She's on her hands and knees with all the other girls, making sure the straw is spread out evenly. There's a guard pacing behind them. He walks along an invisible line, about a hundred feet long, and when he gets to the end of it, he turns around and starts back again. Inka's near the end closest to the canal.

But then this one time, maybe twenty feet after he passes her, the girl to Inka's left, who's looking past Inka toward the guard, bumps Inka on the hip with her hip. And then, so fast that all I see is a flash of orange, Inka grabs a carrot from under the hay and sticks it down the top of her shirt. A second later I'm not even sure the whole thing happened.

"Jiri," I whisper.

"Huh?"

"Inka just . . ."

"Just what?" he asks, not sounding very interested.

"There's . . . there's a carrot in her shirt. She put a carrot in her shirt."

Jiri grins but doesn't stop raking. "Way to go, Inka. Nice, pretty, and one of the slickest *schlojsers* we've got."

"Slickest what?" I ask.

"Schlojsers," he says.

"What the heck is a schlojser?"

"Kapr," Jiri says, "tell Misha what schlojsing is."

Kapr stands up straight and uses his rake to pull out some dirt clumps from the bottom of his shoe. He checks to see that our guard isn't nearby. "If you're delivering bread, and a roll happens to wind up in one of your pockets, that's schlojsing."

"*Happens to wind up?*" I ask. "What's that supposed to mean?"

"How am I supposed to know?" Kapr shrugs his shoulders in this exaggerated way. "I was delivering bread, and the next thing I knew, this roll—okay two rolls—wound up in my pocket."

And then I feel like someone suddenly smacked me in the side of the head. "Stealing? Schlojsing is stealing?"

"No," Jiri says, like I'm a little dense. "Stealing is stealing. Schlojsing is schlojsing."

"What's the difference?" I ask.

"Misha," Kapr says, starting up his raking again. "Let me ask you something. When you showed up in our room for the first time, which bags did you have with you?"

"Uh." I try to remember. It seems like two years ago, even though it hasn't even been a week. "Just my backpack. Why?"

"The rest got delivered later, right?"

"Yeah, I guess."

"So why do you think that was? Because the Nazis run Terezin like a five-star hotel?"

"Your bags, sir," Jiri says in a silly voice.

"I don't know," I say.

"Because when you got here, like everyone else, your stuff went through the *Schleuse*."

A guard paces past us, so no one says anything for a while. We just start raking instead.

Jiri starts up again. "Anything valuable you had in your bag—"

"But I didn't have anything valuable."

"But if you did," Jiri says, "and a lot of people did, then—"

Kapr snaps his finger. "The Nazis make sure it doesn't get to you here. That's what the Schleuse is for."

I keep raking, though I realize I'm not really raking, just moving the thing over the same patch of dirt again and again. "So what does that have to do with her? With"—I lower my voice—"with what she just did?"

"They have their Schleuse, we have ours," Kapr says.

"But it's stealing. That carrot—now whoever was supposed to get it isn't going to get it. And what if she gets caught? What happens then?"

"If you're good," Kapr says, "you don't get caught."

The next thing I know, I'm picturing this time Father and I went to King of Railroads. Everyone was crowding around a new track they had set up that morning. But because I'm so short, I didn't even bother joining them. I knew I wouldn't be able to see a thing. So I just went over to another, smaller table, where I pushed a tiny black caboose back and forth, until, suddenly my hand was putting it in my pants pocket. A second later Father grabbed my wrist. I looked up at him, and the expression on his face made me want to disappear. Just like that we were standing on the sidewalk. I don't know what happened to the caboose, but it definitely wasn't in my hand or my pocket by the time we got outside.

"Michael Gruenbaum," he said in this calm voice that was somehow much worse than him screaming. "If I *ever* see you do that again . . ."

"I won't," I said, my voice all messed up. "I won't." And we walked home in total silence.

"Misha"—Kapr taps the back of my head—"at least pretend you're raking, okay?"

"But," I mumble, "but back in Prague . . . I mean . . . schlojsing . . . whatever you call it . . . it's stealing."

"Yeah, maybe it is," Kapr says. "But this place, if you haven't figured it out by now, this place is definitely not Prague."

December 1, 1942

"APEL!" FRANTA SHOUTS, WALKING BACK and forth between all our beds. "Apel in ten minutes!"

Jiri crawls over me and gets out. I know I need to get up, but I'm so tired. I'm still not sleeping so great here. Was up half the night again listening to everyone's groaning. And a few were crying this time too. Not to mention the bedbugs or the fleas or whatever those were that were biting me all night.

"Nine minutes!" Franta shouts.

Plus it's so freezing, I can almost see my breath. My blanket might be thin, but it's warmer than nothing.

A couple of minutes later I get up fast and pull on my pants and shoes, since the floor might as well be covered in ice.

The bathroom is packed, and I get in line for a sink, even though the lines for the toilets are shorter. But

Franta barely approved me last night, and I'm not taking any chances this time.

He calls out the minute again, but there's too much noise for me to hear the number. I reach the sink and get to work on my nails with the cold water. The dirt is pretty much impossible to remove from under them. It would be much easier if we actually had some soap.

"Misha," someone annoyed behind me says. Gorila, I think. "Hurry up already." I splash my face and rub my ears a few times. Hopefully that will be enough.

"Hands out, palms up," Franta says. And we do as he says, all of us lined up shoulder to shoulder in front of our beds. It sort of feels like we're in the army and Franta's our commander. He walks slowly down the aisle, arms crossed over his chest, peering down at our hands. Sometimes he stops and turns a boy's hands over, sometimes he just keeps going.

I'm sure he'll stop at me.

"Much better today," he tells Pavel, who is standing only two boys away.

Franta gets to me. And I was right. He stops. Takes both my hands, turns them over. Bends down to inspect my nails. I got most of the dirt, but not all. Even though I tried.

"Misha," Franta says.

"Yes," I answer, trying to sound confident.

"I am glad you are working in the gardens. It's good to have a job, and even better to have one outside. The work will keep you strong. Your mother must be a very capable woman to have arranged this for you so quickly after your arrival. But the garden is dirty work, and we cannot have dirt in this room. We simply cannot. There may be tiny creatures living in that dirt, and we already have too many creatures living in Room Seven. Wouldn't you agree?"

"Yes," I answer, and nod my head quickly.

"Mendel has developed an excellent technique for the nails, which he can show you. After you clean the bathrooms."

A few boys giggle. Franta pats me on the shoulder. I stare angrily at the stupid brown lines under my nails and tell myself I better not cry. Far down the line I hear the giggling continue, and then someone says what sounds like "Kid's a total slob."

Franta, still standing right in front of me, freezes. "Who said that?" he asks, not turning in the direction of the voice. No one answers. "Who called Misha a slob?" Again, no answer. Franta doesn't move an inch. He doesn't say a word. And even though he must be angry, he doesn't look it. More like sad, actually.

Ten seconds pass. At least. The giggling dies down, but still no one says a word. Total silence. Franta definitely looks sad at this point.

"Misha," he says calmly, still not moving, "is not a slob. He's a boy who joined the Nesharim eleven days ago. Twelve days ago he was living in Prague. Prague, not Terezin. With his mother and his sister. Now his mother and sister are over in the Dresden Barracks, and he's a prisoner here like the rest of us. He works in the garden and his hands get dirty. Mendel will teach him how to get the dirt out from under his nails. Misha is trying his best. He is not a slob."

Franta looks at me briefly, though there's no expression on his face. No one else talks.

"Do you know what will happen if there is an outbreak of typhus in this room?" He lifts his head back up and pauses for a bit. "When we are underfed and packed together like this? Most every last one of us will get sick. Fever, rashes, and terrible, terrible, terrible headaches. Some of us will get better. But some will not. Some will die. And do you know what the Germans will do if a truly serious outbreak attacks our room? They will isolate us, because even they are afraid of typhus. A big sign on our door—or perhaps even the entire building: *Achtung—Infektionsgefahr*. And then they will wait. Two weeks, three weeks, perhaps even a month. Until every last one of us has either recovered or died. The more who die, the better for them. If the final score is typhus forty, Nesharim nothing, they won't care one bit. No, just the opposite. They will celebrate."

Franta looks down the line, toward the direction of the giggling, which seems like it happened an hour ago.

"So the Nazis want us to make fun of each other. They want us to call each other 'slob' and 'lazy' and 'weak' and 'stupid.' And things much, much worse than that. Oh, what they'd pay to hear one of you call another a dirty Jew. Because instead of supporting one another, instead of loving each other like brothers—and you are all brothers now—they want us to mock each other. This will make us hate ourselves. This will make us weak. And the weaker we are the easier their work becomes. The weaker we are, the harder it will be to fight the typhus when it comes."

Franta looks down to the floor and his eyebrows come together, almost like he's trying to remember something. Then he clears his throat, rubs his face, and inhales deeply. Half the boys are still holding their hands out.

"The Nazis do not believe we are humans. They believe we are something less. They believe we are animals. Why else would they crowd us together like cattle? But they are wrong!" Franta crosses his arms while that last word echoes back and forth. "We will let nothing separate us from our humanity. Not their insults, not their edicts, not their camps. Our duty here is to survive, and survive as human beings. Not as animals. This is our duty to ourselves, and to our parents. We must be ready for life when this ends, because it will. It must. When Misha returns to Prague"—he points at me—"and Pavel to Ostrava, and I to Brno, we all must return as human beings, as people still capable of respecting and loving others."

Franta smiles and begins walking down the line, his hands behind his back. He sort of sways from side to side.

"So, no, Misha is not a slob. He is a young man doing his very best here. And after breakfast"—he points at a couple of boys down near the end of the line—"Hanus and Kurt, you two gigglers will show Misha that the Nesharim excel in all areas. Including the cleaning of toilets. Now, all of you, off to breakfast."

December 13, 1942

"I'M SORRY YOUR WORK IN THE GARDEN is over," Mother says, "but I'm hopeful you'll return there come springtime. That is, if we're still here then. But so, tell me. How is school going?" I'm sitting across from Marietta at a long table in their room in the Dresden Barracks. Well, it's obviously not just their room, because this place is packed with triple-decker bunk beds too. There might even be more people living here than back in Room 7. Right now the place feels only half full, but still, women are all over the room, reading, napping, sewing, cleaning, or chatting.

It's like this most evenings, which is when I usually come to visit. Because it turns out that we can go pretty much anywhere we want whenever we want. Inside Terezin, that is, and so long as we don't have somewhere particular Franta wants us to be. And, of course, so long as we're back before curfew, because no one can be out after that.

"It's not school," I tell her, swallowing the last bite of a small, delicious pastry she somehow got her hands on. I could eat another hundred like it, even though there was finally a bit of salami with dinner tonight. "It's called the Program. School's not allowed. That's why some days I have to stand guard out front. Remember? In case an SS officer comes to the building."

"Which would never happen," Marietta says. "So long as we don't cause any trouble, the Nazis couldn't care less about what we do here. I haven't seen one of those monsters since we arrived."

Mother's behind us, doing something to their bed, though I can't figure out what.

"Well, okay, so what did you learn in the Program today?" she asks. Marietta puts down a jack of clubs, but I don't remember what that means. She's teaching me some new card game she learned here that she said I ought to show everyone.

"Today"—I try to remember—"Professor Kohn—"

"Professor?" Mother asks.

"Yeah, I guess he was a professor in Prague. He gave us a math lesson."

"Ugh, math," Marietta says. "I'm glad I have to work in the laundry all day."

"It wasn't that bad," I say. "We don't have much to

write on, so he taught us a song to help us remember the order of operations."

"How does it go?" Mother asks.

"Forget it," I say, and put down the ten of diamonds. Marietta moves the card under two of her cards already out on the table. Her fingertips are pale and wrinkled, which isn't what they used to look like. It must be because of her work.

Mother lifts up a corner of their mattress and yanks out the edge of a blanket. "Okay, so after Professor Kohn, then what?"

"Uh, then Professor Zwicker—"

"Another professor," Mother says.

"He gave us a lecture about Czech history."

"Was it interesting?" she asks.

"It was okay."

"What did he tell you?"

I pretend to rack my memory, but what I'm really thinking about is what happened right after his lecture. Professor Zwicker told us we'd have an exam on Thursday, and then he left. Franta left too, because he said he had to go check about practice times with Jacob, the other madrich. Dr. Jelinkova was supposed to come next to teach us English, but she was late for some reason. So there we were, waiting, when all of a sudden I heard two weird noises, one right after the other, coming from the other side of the room. The first was kind of a *poof* sound, the other was more like a thud.

I looked over. Gorila was lying on the ground with a dazed smile on his face. Standing over him was Jila, with a pillow in his hand and a much larger smile on his face.

Gorila sprung back up, grabbed a pillow, and whacked Jila hard in his side. Not two seconds later, every single boy in the room had joined in. Twenty, thirty, forty pillows swinging through the air. Jiri had a pillow in each hand and walked down the length of the table, bashing anyone within reach. Felix straddled two ladders and nailed Brena when he tried to run beneath him. Erich and Koko ganged up on Petr, who giggled and crawled quickly down the tunnel of middle bunks in their row.

I just stood near the front of the room, both hands wrapped tight around the end of my pillow, which wasn't actually my pillow, waiting for someone to attack. Brena nailed Felix in the side of the head so hard his pillow ripped open. Along with feathers, a weird combination of straw and wood shavings started pouring out. Felix grabbed a bunch and stuffed it down Brena's shirt. Right around then I noticed clouds of feathers popping up in other spots of the room. A couple of seconds later I was spinning around and giggling, the pillow cocked behind my shoulder, when I noticed Franta standing in the doorway, his arms crossed over his chest.

I froze and let the pillow slide out of my hands and onto the floor. Without looking like I was running, I made my way through all those feathers and returned as quickly as possible to the stool I was sitting on before.

Franta slammed the door. "Nesharim!" he shouted. A few of the boys noticed, but not all, because the rest of the room was total chaos. "Nesharim!!!" Franta yelled even louder, marching toward a clump of boys still bashing each other with whatever was left of their pillows. A few seconds later the pillow fight was definitely over, even though some feathers continued floating in the air.

"Have you all gone mad?" Franta asked, his face red. "Where do you think you are? Do you think this is a resort?" No one said anything. "What are we going to do with all these feathers? How will we get them back into your pillows? And how will you sleep without pillows? And what if insects were happily living inside your pillows? Where do you think they are going to live now? And what if, *what if* an SS officer happened to be walking below our window at this moment, perhaps in the camp today for an inspection of some sort? Why, why would you ever do anything to draw attention to yourselves? I heard your racket from the other end of the hall. Do you not think Terezin provides enough challenges to us each and every day? Was it really necessary to create more?"

No one said a word. Franta made a small pile of feathers and wood shavings with his shoe.

"This, all of this, is to be cleaned up within five minutes. And after that, since Dr. Jelinkova is sick, we will have rehearsal instead."

"But we have rehearsal tonight," Pavel said.

Uh-oh, that's right, I remember now, looking at my mother. Rehearsal.

I totally forgot.

"What time is it?" I ask Mother.

"I don't know," she says. "Why?"

I stand up. "I've got to go."

"What?" Mother says. "You only just arrived."

"But we have rehearsal for our play. It probably already started."

Marietta shuffles the cards. "Play? What play?" she asks.

"*The Pied Piper*," I say, buttoning up my jacket.

"Is the play a secret too?" Mother asks. "Like your school?"

"Uh, I'm not sure," I say, heading toward the door. "We're just rehearsing right now."

"Remember," Marietta hollers to me, "the ace can be high or low."

"Hold on, hold on, Misha," Mother says. I turn around. She's holding a folded-up blanket in her hands. I recognize the pattern; it's the blanket she and Father used to sleep under back in Prague. "Here, take this."

"What?"

"Take it. Winter is coming."

"What about us?" Marietta asks. "That's our heavy blanket."

"Greta says she saw two flannel blankets in the attic this morning, we can use those instead."

"But," Marietta says, "those won't be nearly—"

"I can't take it," I say.

"What are you talking about, you can't take it?" Mother asks.

"It's not fair," I say. "No one else has a blanket like that."

Mother deposits it into my arms. "But you will, and that's all that matters."

"No," I say, pushing it back to her. "It's not fair. Anyway, Franta won't allow it."

"Franta," Mother says, almost laughing, "Franta's not your Mother. He doesn't get to decide. I'll come with you right now and talk to him myself."

"Don't," I say, even more firmly than I wanted to, and from the look on Mother's face I might as well have slapped her. "Sorry. Just don't. I'll talk to him about it," I tell her, even though I know I won't. "Okay?"

Mother holds the blanket against her chest, her cheeks red. I look over at Marietta, who just shakes her head. From the corner of my eye I notice a few women staring at us. I take a couple of steps toward Mother and hug her. When she doesn't let go right away, I let my head sink deeper in between the folds of the blanket, where I swear I can smell our old apartment back in Holesovice.

The smell wants me to stay like this forever, but I yank my head out instead. "Thanks for the pastry," I tell Mother. Before she can respond, I'm out the door. Hopefully Franta won't be mad at me for being late.

After rehearsal I'm washing up when Franta comes in. Somehow we're the only two in here. I look over at him, but he's looking at the floor for some reason. Then he bends over and picks something up. A feather.

Franta turns it back and forth in between his fingers. "We'll be finding these for the next month," he says, shaking his head.

"Sorry," I say, and start walking back to the room,

scanning the floor to see if there are any other feathers we missed.

"Misha," he calls out to me when I'm almost to the doorway.

"Yeah?" I say, and turn around.

"It was fun, wasn't it?" he asks.

"What?"

"The pillow fight," he says.

I don't know how to answer, or what he wants me to say. I search his eyes, looking for a clue. Is he testing me?

"Uh, yeah, kind of."

"Kind of?" His eyes soften a bit.

"Yes, it was. It was really fun."

"I bet it was," he says, a small smile on his face. "I bet it was." I don't say anything, just watch him stare at the floor, clearly thinking about something, who knows what.

"Lots of things are fun here," I say. "Soccer, even play rehearsal. I mean, I don't know why my mother kept trying to get us off the transports here."

Franta laughs, though it's not exactly a laugh. Maybe just a sigh.

"What?" I ask.

"Nothing."

"What?"

"I'm glad you're able to enjoy yourself here. I wish that

could somehow be a more common experience in this rotten place."

"What do you mean?" I ask.

Franta's smile continues to grow, but his eyes don't match it at all. "Nothing, Misha," he says. "It doesn't mean anything. Please forget I said it. And now, to bed. It's late. Tomorrow's another day."

"Good night, Franta."

"Good night, Misha," he says.

And soon I'm back in bed, where I fall asleep almost instantly, even though my pillow is half the size it was this morning.

December 28, 1942

I WAS SO EXCITED WHEN THE SUN CAME out today and Franta told us we'd be having practice, but then I just played awful.

"I stink," I say to Jiri as we head down the bashta and back to L417.

"No you don't," Jiri says, but I can tell he's just trying to be nice.

"What are you talking about? I haven't scored a single goal since I've been here."

"So?" Jiri says. "I barely ever score."

"You're a defender, Jiri. Defenders aren't supposed to score. I play wing; wings are—"

"Uh-oh," Jiri says, turning around, "I forgot my hat."

I stand there for a moment, trying to figure out why this place makes me so bad at soccer. But then, when Jiri doesn't come back right away, I head back up to the bashta. He's talking to Franta, who's folding up a piece of paper and putting it in his pocket. The two of them give me a look that makes it pretty clear what, or who, they were talking about. I pretend I don't notice. Pretty soon the three of us are walking back down again.

"Jiri, Misha," Franta says as we walk under some trees. "Do me a favor; grab a bunch of twigs."

"How many?" I ask.

"A bunch," he says.

"Why?" Jiri asks.

"Just pick some up."

We do what he says and soon we have a few dozen, some long, some short, most a little crooked. Franta sits down on a bench, so we join him, the twigs in our hands.

"Jiri," Franta says, "hand me a twig." Franta takes one of the longer sticks from Jiri and holds it out in front of us. "What do you think will happen if I try to bend this?"

"It'll break," I say.

"Exactly," Franta says, and snaps it in half. "Jiri, two more please." Jiri gives him two shorter ones, and Franta holds them together in front of us. "What now?" he asks.

Jiri and I look at each other. "Same thing." Jiri says it almost like a question.

Franta snaps both of them in half. "Misha, give me . . . give me eleven twigs." One at a time, I hand him eleven.

He takes them and arranges them in a little bundle. "Now what?" I shrug my shoulders. "Do you think I'll be able to break them?"

"Yeah?" Jiri says.

Franta grips the sticks tight, making the tendons on the back of his hands bulge. He's really not that big, but his hands are incredibly strong. The funny thing, he actually is a goalie, just like I thought the day I met him. I haven't seen him play yet, but all the kids say he's amazing. Totally fearless. It's been too cold, but when it warms up they'll start the league again. The adult one, where the different work groups play each other. I guess the teachers, which include Franta, are one of the very best teams.

Franta's knuckles are growing white, but the twigs won't break. He lets go. "Here," he says, handing me the sticks. "Give it a try, in case you thought I was pulling your leg."

So I take them and try, even though I doubt Franta would ever pull my leg. "I can't."

"Jiri," Franta says, and Jiri grabs all the sticks. "No, no. Take just one." Jiri does. "Snap it." Jiri does. "Another." Same thing. "Another." Pretty soon twenty-two twigs are lying on the ground in front of us. "Well?" Franta asks.

"You can't break them together," I say, staring at the twigs. "Right?" Franta doesn't say anything. "Right?" I look and notice Franta watching two men walking down a street not that far from us. He follows them with his eyes for a while, not blinking once. One is a Jew, wearing glasses with round frames. The other is a Nazi, an SS officer with a pointy nose and a chin that sticks out. It's only the second time I've seen an SS officer since I've been here. He's just walking slowly, but I shiver for a moment and feel something tighten up in my chest. Even though I can't see every detail from this far away, I'm pretty sure his uniform has the iron cross and the squares and the eagle and the skull, just like the men who came to our apartment and took Father away. I close my eyes and lower my head.

"Who's that?" I whisper to Jiri.

"I think that's Seidl, and . . ."

"Edelstein," Franta says, not looking away.

"Who are they?" I ask.

"Seidl is in charge," Jiri says, "of everything."

"SS Officer Dr. Siegfried Seidl," Franta says quietly, but with disgust, too. "Commandant of Terezin."

"And Edelstein," Jiri says.

"Jakob Edelstein runs the camp for Seidl," Franta says.

"What do you mean, runs it?"

"He's the head of the Jewish Council," Jiri says.

"Huh?" I ask.

"Edelstein oversees the day-to-day operations," Franta says. "So the Nazis don't have to. Just another rotten collaborator, only he has to make impossible decisions, too." I'm about to ask Jiri what "impossible decisions" means when Franta stands up and says, "C'mon, let's go. Literature class starts soon."

A minute later, with L417 not too far off, I ask Franta, "Wait, what was that about with the twigs?"

"Yeah," Jiri adds.

The left edge of Franta's mouth curls up. He looks down and grabs a thin stick near the edge of the street. "Misha, this is you. You're a rather thin stick. For now anyway."

"Okay," I say, feeling kind of stupid.

"Someday you'll be thicker. Someday we all will be. And Jiri," Franta says, "you're a slightly thicker stick. The Gotzlinger brothers, Pudlina and Felix, they're the thickest sticks among all the Nesharim. But still, quite thin all by themselves."

I don't say anything, just look over at Jiri, who appears to be about as confused as me.

"Each of us, by ourselves," Franta says, "doesn't stand much of a chance. Sorry, Misha." And he snaps the stick. "You're a pretty good player. Better than you think you are, in fact. You do a number of things quite well. You don't crowd the ball, you're quick, you always hurry back on defense when there's a counterattack. And you do a great job on throw-ins." He pats my back. "Okay, I'll admit, it's not a World Cup resume, but it's not so bad, because you have plenty to contribute. To the team. You're not playing alone. Remember that. You're playing on a team. Eleven sticks. The Nesharim. Some of us are so-so, some of us are good. Pudlina and Felix, perhaps they are great, but not amazing, not yet anyway. But together we can be great. If we play together."

Franta takes a deep breath and nods his head. Then he starts talking again, quieter and slower than before. "If we truly play together, if we help each other and support each other and make it so each of us does the things he can do, if we make it so each of us trusts that someone else will do the things he can't do himself, if we do that, we will be the best team in our building. That's what I meant."

We start walking again.

"Have you seen Otto Hirsch play?" Franta asks. "From Room One?"

"He's incredible," Jiri says.

"Yes," Franta says, "he's the most skilled player in our building. His footwork is better than some seasoned players twice his age. But he plays with his head down. Please don't repeat this to anyone, but, frankly, he's something of a ball hog. And his teammates wind up standing around and watching. You wait. When we play them, he'll have a hat trick, but we'll win four to three."

I've never been on a real team before. I doubt we'll get uniforms here, since here is Terezin, but still, even just being on a real team will be pretty great. No, it will be better than great. It will be the best thing since . . . since all this started.

Jiri starts running up the stairs to L417, so I race to beat him.

"Wait," Franta calls out, so we stop. His head turns back to where Seidl and Edelstein were walking, even though they're long gone by now. "You must know, however, that the Nazis . . ."

"Huh?" I ask.

"The Nazis, they work together too. Hitler gathered up a lot of sticks. Millions of them." Franta points at a row of trees. "When you see ten thousand people with their arms sticking out, yelling "Heil Hitler" in perfect unison, that's quite a bundle, no? To get all of us to Terezin, to keep us here, in these conditions, to . . . to do what they've done, what they're doing, you need a very, very, *very* large bundle."

"But then," I start to say, "but then what about—"

"So . . . ," Franta says quickly, but then stops again. "So it's not enough to work together. You must always ask yourself, am I in the right bundle? Is this a bundle I want to make stronger by joining it?"

I stare at the trees, a little confused.

"The Nesharim's a good bundle," Jiri says.

"Right?" I ask.

"Yes," Franta says, "I believe it is. I believe the Nesharim make a wonderful bundle." Franta rubs his chin, thinking about something, who knows what. "C'mon, you two sticks," he finally says. "Let's go. The others are going to wonder what happened to us." And he leaps up the stairs, the two of us right behind him.

January 22, 1943

"'OH, POET.'" DR. WEISS READS SOME POEM by a guy named Josef Hora. He reads all dramatically with his hand out in the air. "'I am drowning in the sea of your soul torn by its deepest tide.'" I'm trying to listen for a change today, even though Czech literature is maybe the most boring part of the Program, because sometimes Dr. Weiss stops and makes one of us explain what we think the poem means. I'm hoping this one will end soon, but the morning Program usually lasts from nine until noon, which means we still have a way to go.

Suddenly there's a knock at the door. Everyone freezes for a second, and then quickly hurries to hide anything that might give us away. Because no one knocks around here. Pavel and Hanus, who seem to actually care about literature and bother to take notes, throw their scraps of paper and short, stubby pencils under the nearest mattress.

Dr. Weiss closes the book and stands up, only to sit down right away.

But when the door opens, all that happens is some Jewish woman walks in, all by herself. Maybe Mother's age. Taller than her, in an old dress with a flower pattern on it. Her hair is kind of wavy and frizzy, though she has most of it back in a bun. She closes the door behind her.

"Mom?" Jila says.

Franta stands up the second she came in. "Mrs. Zweig," he says, opening the door again and trying to get her to go back outside with him. But she just stands there, ignoring Franta completely. "Mrs. Zweig," Franta says again, more firmly this time, "I'm sorry, but we're in the middle of a lesson."

"There's a transport, tomorrow," she says, her voice shaking. She hurries over to Jila and hugs him, which I can tell embarrasses him. "We're on it."

Dr. Weiss removes his glasses and rubs his face. Franta sighs loudly but doesn't say anything.

I turn to Pedro, who's sitting next to me. "Transport?" I whisper. "Transport to where?" But he doesn't answer.

In fact, no one says anything for a bit. All of us stare at Jila's mom, who's crying so much she's not even bothering to hide it.

"How many?" Franta finally asks.

She wipes her face with a handkerchief. "Two thousand."

"Two thousand," Dr. Weiss says in a way that makes it pretty clear that was the worst possible answer.

"Tomorrow?" Franta asks.

She nods.

"Everyone," Franta says, "go to the courtyard, now. Go and take the carts, one to the Dresden Barracks, one to the Engineer Barracks. People will need help with their bags, especially the elderly in Engineer."

I have a ton of questions, so I walk over to Franta as soon as everyone gets up, only just then an older man appears, his eyes red.

"Mr. Forman?" Franta asks.

"Pedro," the man says in a panic. "Where's Pedro?"

We're barely outside our building before I can tell this isn't just another day in Terezin. People are rushing all over the place. And everyone has the same expression on their face, like they all know a bad day is about to get much, much worse.

"I don't understand," I say to Felix on our way with the cart to the Engineer Barracks. "Didn't they already transport us here?"

"These go to the East," he says.

"What do you mean, the East?"

He shrugs his shoulders. "How should I know? The East. Poland maybe."

"But why?" I ask. "What's in Poland?"

A man sprints past us, almost running straight into our cart.

"They said it's to go to a labor camp. Some people say it's to some place called Birkenau."

"But this is a labor camp. Isn't it?" I ask. "I mean, that's what they told us when we left Prague, that Terezin . . . that we'd work here and . . . what was it . . . be productive. That's what some SS officer told us all back in Prague anyway. And we are working, even us kids work sometimes. So why do they need to go to another—"

"I don't know, Misha, okay?" Felix said. "So will you shut up about it already?"

The Engineer Barracks are completely out of control. People yelling and trudging down the stairs, most with bags too heavy to carry. Felix and I find a tiny old woman, barely our size, with a worn-out suitcase, so we try to help her. But the thing keeps opening from different sides because all its hinges are broken. Her clothes spill out everywhere. Socks, underwear, and shirts that look like they couldn't possibly belong to her. I think they're men's shirts actually.

And she mumbles the whole time, but I can't understand a thing. Maybe she's talking in another language.

By the time we get back to our cart, it's already over-flowing with bags. We stuff most of the woman's things back into her suitcase and jam it between the side of the cart and another bag so it won't open again. We have to get Pavel and Hanus to help, but we finally manage to get the cart rolling. Going about one mile per hour, we head toward the Hamburg Barracks, near where the Schleuse is.

A couple of minutes later I look around and notice that the cart's working like a magnet. There must be thirty old women trailing behind us. Each one looks more exhausted than the last. And then I think, wait, what good will any of them do at a different labor camp? Because it's not like they're doing any work here.

"Hey," I say to Felix, who's pushing right next to me. "Where is she?"

"She?"

"That woman. With the broken suitcase. I don't see her."

Before Felix can respond, I let go of the cart and head back to find her. It takes a bit, but eventually I spot her, sitting on a bench by herself in the middle of nowhere. I sit down next to her. She smells like an old mop. I try to think of something to say but can't come up with a single thing. I doubt she'd answer anyway, since she's just staring ahead like she's in some kind of trance, her tiny head tilted really far to one side.

So after a while I get up and rush back to the cart.

January 23, 1943

"LOOK, THERE'S JILA," KAPR SAYS ALL excited, pointing through the window of the Schleuse. "Jila! Hey, Jila!"

But Jila doesn't hear, probably because of the noise everywhere.

"Jila! Jila!"

In fact, I can hardly hear Kapr screaming, and he's standing right next to me. There are hundreds of people on the other side of the window, most of them sitting on the ground with their bags. The whole thing looks a lot like the Exhibition Hall did a couple of months back, only everyone seems even sadder here, which I didn't think could ever be possible. But everyone seems pretty sure that being on a transport leaving Terezin is way worse than being on one headed here.

"Jila! Jila! JILA!!!"

* * *

"Jila! Jiiiillllllaaaa!" Kapr yells for the tenth time, his hands cupped around his mouth. Somehow Jila finally hears us and heads over.

"Hey," he says, his hands on the thick cement windowsill.

Kapr takes a deck of cards out of his pants pocket and passes it through the metal bars. "Take these. In case you get bored on the train."

"Okay," Jila says, "thanks."

"And I saved this roll from lunch," Kapr says. "Here." And he extends a half-smushed roll toward Jila.

"No, I don't need it," Jila says. "My mom got a whole loaf from some lady in the bakery."

"All right," Kapr says, and takes a bite from the roll.

Jila looks at me, and I wonder if I was supposed to bring something too. But honestly, I barely know him. I only came here because Kapr told me I should.

"When do you leave?" Kapr asks him.

Jila shrugs his shoulders. "No idea. Tonight. Tomorrow. Hopefully never. My mom keeps trying to find out, but no one seems to know for sure."

Kapr grabs one of the bars and sort of yanks on it. "You'll still get off I bet," he tells Jila.

"Nah," Jila says.

"But you said your mom knows someone who works with mica."

"Who's Mica?" I ask.

"Not who, what," Kapr says. "It's some kind of material they use to make stuff that goes into guns or radios or something. Anyone who works with that stuff is safe."

Mother just works in some place sewing up toys and fake flowers. She told me she's starting to really get the hang of it, but still, is that safe?

"*Knows* someone," Jila says. "How does knowing someone help?"

"I don't know," Kapr says, "maybe they need someone. Maybe someone working over there got caught schlojsing and so got put on the transport and maybe your mom can replace her. Right?"

"Maybe," Jila says, not sounding too convinced.

"Get lost, you two." There's a hand on my shoulder. I turn and see a man wearing a black cap with a yellow band around it. *Ghettowache*, a ghetto guard, even though he has a yellow star on his chest like everyone else. Franta would call him another rotten collaborator, I bet.

I start walking off as fast as I can, but then Kapr says, "We're just talking."

The man grabs the back of Kapr's jacket and throws him to the ground. "Now," he says.

Kapr gets up and brushes some dirt off. "Jila," he says, "when we get back to Prague, we'll—"

"Go!" the guard screams. "Unless you want to join him. Which can easily be arranged." He actually sounds happy saying it. I swear, if he didn't have that star on his chest, I'd bet he was a Nazi himself. Rotten, definitely rotten.

About ten steps later, I turn back toward the Schleuse. Jila's already gone.

Pretty soon I can barely hear the Schleuse behind us.

"Stupid guard," Kapr says, throwing something, the rest of his roll maybe, at a tree.

"Kapr," I say.

"Huh?"

"Where do you think they're going?" He picks up a rock and throws it at another tree. "I mean, do you think that maybe, maybe it won't be so bad? Because it would be pretty hard for a place to be worse than here, right? Because in a lot of ways this place is even worse than Prague was at the end. You know?" I ask, not sure if I'm saying all of this just to make him feel better or because I actually believe it. "Not enough food and living in a room crammed with about ten times too many people where fleas bite you all night long. The whole place surrounded by high walls covered in grass. And old people dying all the time. Not to mention," I say, beginning to feel that I believe all this a little more than I wish I did, "they can just order any of us onto a transport whenever they want. With no warning at all. So, you know, maybe where they're going won't be so bad. Maybe it'll be better. Maybe it's just because it's so crowded here, and wherever they're going there's more space. Maybe that's the only reason. Maybe you don't ever have to leave wherever they're all going, at least not until the war finally ends. And maybe, maybe," I say, trying hard to cheer myself up, "maybe they'll even have real soccer fields there and Jila will be able to start a version of the Nesharim team there."

Kapr looks at me but doesn't answer.

"Guys! Guys!" someone yells to us. I turn around. It's Pedro.

"Hey, what are you doing?" I ask.

"We got off! It worked! My dad got us off!"

"That's great," Kapr says, and looks like he's about to say something else, but then turns around and quickly walks on ahead of us.

Pedro doesn't seem to notice, just says, "My uncle works in the finance department, and he knows Edelstein's assistant, and, well, we got off!"

Just then Kapr starts running, but for some reason turns right, which is the opposite direction from our building. Pedro and I take off after him. A couple of minutes later we find him inside the arched doorway of another building, his arms crossed, his head pressed against the smooth, hard wall.

"Kapr," I say, "c'mon, let's go. Franta told us to be back soon. We should hurry up." He doesn't say anything, just turns farther away from us.

"Yeah," Pedro says, reaching out his arm and putting it on Kapr's shoulder.

"Just leave me alone!" Kapr screams, and then his whole back starts shaking.

"Do you think," I ask Pedro when we're almost at our building, "do you think that two thousand means exactly two thousand?"

"I don't know. Maybe. Probably."

"Because," I say, feeling the words come out of my mouth but not being too happy about it, "the Germans, they seem pretty serious about things being really organized, right?"

"Yeah," Pedro says.

"And so I bet it does. Mean exactly two thousand."

"So what?" Pedro says.

"Forget it," I say.

"What?"

"Never mind."

"What, Misha?"

"Just that, you know, doesn't that mean that some other people will have to go instead of your family? Now that you're off."

Pedro doesn't answer. We walk another minute or so until we get to L417. He opens the door, but then stops before going inside. "So long as it's not us," he says real fast, "I don't care. I don't."

We're heading down our hallway upstairs, when I see a familiar body from behind.

Mother. What's she doing here?

I run quickly ahead, but she turns around before I reach her. She's holding that blanket in her hands again.

"Misha," she says, smiling weakly.

"Hi," I say. And I'm about to say something else, I'm not sure what, when the door to our room opens and Franta steps out.

"You're late," he says to me, not happy at all. "I told you"—he checks his watch—"to be here fifteen minutes ago. And where's Kapr?"

"Hey, Franta," Pedro says casually when he reaches us, like the whole thing was a joke he played on everyone.

"Pedro!" Franta's eyes light up. He reaches his hand out and messes up Pedro's hair. "You got off, you got off!"

Then he pulls Pedro to him and gives him a big hug. "Welcome back, my friend, welcome back."

"My uncle did it!"

"I see, I see. That's wonderful. Now get inside. I was about to read to everyone."

Pedro disappears, leaving just the three of us.

"A horrible day," Mother says, still clutching the blanket. Franta nods and rubs his face. "I brought this for Misha," she says, "until it warms up a bit."

"Misha," Franta says, "why don't you go inside and wash up?"

I look back and forth at the two of them, not sure what to do. Should I take the blanket? Should I see if Mother is going to tell me to go inside like Franta said? While I'm standing there, Kapr comes running down the hall and disappears inside the room before Franta can even say a word to him, leaving me to continue staring at the two of them. In the end, I hug her without moving my feet and go inside. But then, after closing the door, I stick my ear to it, plugging my other ear with my thumb.

"Mrs. Gruenbaum, I—" Franta says.

"I want him to have it," she says. "Half the boys in this room have been sick since we got here two months ago. And if we get called on the next transport, he needs to be well."

And even though maybe I realized it was a possibility since yesterday, hearing Mother actually say it, that *we* could be on a transport, it makes my stomach tighten up like a small fist. What if there are three people in Pedro's family and so we get called instead? Because this place might not be perfect, but I don't want to leave, that's all I know.

"In fact," I hear Franta say through the door, "we've had only eight illnesses requiring medical attention since the start of December. You should know that the boys spend a great deal of time every day cleaning—"

"Franta," Mother says, "listen to me. I appreciate what you do. I know Misha adores you. But I am his mother. His mother. And you, there's a great deal you don't know. About our family. About being a parent. You cannot—"

"Mrs. Gruenbaum, my job at this camp is your son. Your son and thirty-seven, no, thirty-eight, other sons. This is what I do, all day, every day. My workday, unlike yours, has no end."

"That's not fair, Franta, you—"

"When the decision was made to house children separately, the decision was also made that the madrichs would have final authority. If you give Misha that blanket, other boys will—"

"I don't care about the other boys! I care ab—"

"And that's why I'm in charge, and you're not."

"How dare you! I'm not some—"

"I'm sorry, just a moment," Franta says. Suddenly the door opens and I stumble into the hallway. "Misha," he says to me, "wash up and get into bed. Now."

A couple of minutes later the door opens. It's Franta. Alone and without the blanket.

"It's been a long day," he announces to the room. "But if you're quiet and promise not to complain in the morning, I'll read an extra five minutes tonight."

If I had to guess, I'd say he read an extra ten minutes, maybe even fifteen. But it doesn't really matter, because a half hour later I can still hear Kapr, alone in the bed he used to share with Jila, crying himself to sleep.

July 7, 1943

"MISHA." FRANTA POINTS TO ME AT THE end of practice.

"Yes?" All of us are sitting in a tight circle. Franta stands in the middle, quizzing us on strategy.

"What do you do if Petr is on the attack and coming right at you?" This practice was about ten times more serious than any practice so far, and we've had some pretty serious practices.

"Petr Adler?" I ask.

"No, Peter Pan," Franta says, clearly annoyed. A few of the other boys laugh.

Of course this practice was more serious, we've made the finals. We actually made the finals, I still can't believe it. Came from behind to beat Room 9, 4–3. Now we get to play Room 1. They have Otto Hirsch *and* Zdenek Taussig, who are both better than anyone we have. They clobbered Room 5, 7–2.

I wipe some sweat out of my eyes. Today's got to be the hottest day since I've been here. "I force him to the sideline."

"Exactly," Franta says, nodding his head. "Exactly. On defense the sideline is your teammate. Don't give them the middle of the field. Don't ever give them the middle of the field. The middle is ours." Franta turns and points at someone else. "Koko."

"Yeah," he answers.

"They have a corner kick. You're in goal. You don't like where Pavel and Jiri are standing. What do you do?"

"I tell them."

"Tell them?" Franta asks, raising his eyebrows.

"Yeah," Koko says, "I tell them."

"No, you shout at them! 'Pavel, you're on Otto! No, other side! On his right! Jiri, two steps back! Now! Go!' You're in charge back there. It's not a time for manners. And all of you, talk to each other out there. Communicate. If we play as a team"—Franta makes a fist—"we win. If we play as individuals, we lose. It's that simple." He crosses his arms, stretching the dark oval of sweat on the back of his shirt into something closer to a circle. "Everyone, in."

We get up and cluster around him. Pavel, Felix,

Pudlina, Koko, Gorila, Pedro, Jiri, Leo, Hanus, Majoshek, Erich, Grizzly, Kapr, and me.

"Rim, rim, rim, tempo Nesharim," Franta whispers, and extends his hand. Everyone whispers it back and puts a hand on top of his. "Rim, rim, rim, tempo Nesharim," he says, a little louder this time.

"Rim, rim, rim, tempo Nesharim," we answer.

"Rim, rim, rim, tempo Nesharim!" he says.

"Rim, rim, rim, tempo Nesharim!"

"Rim, rim, rim, tempo Nesharim!"

"Rim, rim, rim, tempo Nesharim!"

And then nothing but the sound of our voices slowly echoing back to us from the far wall of this stupid prison fortress.

"Great practice," Franta says. "Now back to the room to wash up. And then everyone, meet in the basement of the girls' barracks in twenty minutes."

"What's there?" Gorila asks.

"Something new," Franta says, "now go."

"We're going to destroy Room One," Felix says on our way back.

"I'd be glad just winning by one," Pavel says.

"Yeah," Erich says.

We cross the train tracks, the new train tracks

running all the way into the camp. Just a week ago the first train arrived on them. A short one, carrying maybe a hundred Jews. And then a few days later, another with the same amount. Someone said they were both from Berlin. No one was transported to the East on either train when they pulled out of here, but still, it's not like they'd lay these tracks just to bring in a couple hundred people.

We walk along the rail, all of us in a line, until we reach the end.

Thank God Franta said the basement and not the attic. The air down here is kind of heavy and tastes like dust and spiderwebs, but at least it's cool. There's a lot of kids sitting on the floor, including girls, all of us facing the front of the room. I notice Inka and her red hair off to one side. And like most everywhere else around here, it's extremely loud.

"Children, children, quiet down!" a madricha, which is what they call a madrich if she's not a man, says. It takes a while, but eventually the room is almost quiet. There are two older men up near the front of the room with her. Both have thick dark hair, and the skinnier one has a widow's peak. The other one looks a little sleepy.

"I'm Resi," the madricha says. "Hello."

Some of the kids say hello back, though not me or Jiri, who's sitting next to me.

"How many of you," Resi asks, taking her long brown braid and tossing it over her shoulder, "have participated in a choir or a play since you've been here?" I put my hand up, like most of the other kids here. "Helga"—the woman points at a girl off to one side—"what have you been in?"

"A choir," some girl I can't see says. "We sing songs in Czech, and some in Hebrew, too."

"Good," the madricha says. "Good. What about plays—who's been in a play?" Along with a ton of other kids I put my hand up. For some reason, the Nazis don't care if we put on plays; I still don't know why. Suddenly I realize Resi is actually pointing at me. "Yes, and what was the name of it?"

"*The Pied Piper of Hamelin*," I say, glad she didn't ask what role I had, since I was just one of the rats, and then one of the kids. Though I did play an instrument too. Well, not a real instrument. Just a comb with a piece of toilet paper wrapped around it. But it actually sounded pretty good.

"Excellent, excellent. Now, does anyone know what you call it when you combine a choir with a play?" There's a lot of murmuring, but no one raises their hand. "No one knows?" Resi asks with a grin on her face. "Lilka, I know you know."

"An opera?" a girl with curly hair near the front says.

"Exactly, an opera," Resi says, and looks over at the two men, who don't seem too interested in our conversation. "Well, guess what? We're going to perform an opera. A children's opera." More murmuring and even some laughs. "This"—she points at the man with the widow's peak—"this is Rafael Schaechter, a pianist and composer." The man nods his head slightly. "Did any of you see *The Bartered Bride*? The opera by . . . ?"

"Smetana," Schaechter says, and nods his head slowly.

"Did any of you see it?" Resi asks us. A few kids raise their hand. "Too bad more of you couldn't see it, because it was truly wonderful. Well, Mr. Schaechter was in charge of that production here. And now he's agreed to be the musical director for a children's opera—"

A bunch of kids start talking, and a bunch of others laugh. Schaechter leans over to the other man and whispers something to him.

"Children, children!" Resi shouts. "Please. Please quiet down." Eventually the room gets quieter, but not really quiet. "This opera is called *Brundibar*."

"Brundibar?" Jiri says to me, like she just said "underwear."

Schaechter gets up from his chair and walks over to a small, brown piano near the back of the room. He opens the lid and runs his fingers along the keys, but doesn't actually play anything. Then he starts playing a song. It almost sounds like a merry-go-round, but then it speeds up, or, I don't know, it sounds like a merry-go-round if the horses were trying to break free. Schaechter closes his eyes and begins humming along to the piano. He hums softly, but I can hear him clearly, because now the room is completely silent. For some reason I close my eyes.

Eventually the piano stops, and I open my eyes. Resi points at the other man. "This is Rudolf Freudenfeld. He will be our director. Rudolf, would you tell them what *Brundibar* is about?"

He stands up and begins pacing in front of us, not looking tired at all anymore. His hands go up like he's a magician. "There are two children, Aninka and Pepichek. They are brother and sister. Their father is gone. And their mother is ill. Very ill. The doctor comes one day and says, 'She will only get better if she drinks milk.' But they have no money. Why, they are nearly orphans! What will they do?" He looks over at Schaechter, like he's expecting him to answer, but Schaechter seems more interested in the piano. "They decide to sing in the marketplace. To raise money. But the evil organ-grinder, Brundibar"—he says the name like it tastes bad—"keeps chasing them away. Brundibar is a terrible man with a mustache—"

"A terrible man with a mustache," Jiri leans over and whispers to me. "Sound familiar?"

"What will they do? They need money. Well, lucky for Aninka and Pepichek, a sparrow, a cat, and a dog, along with the other children of the town, they help them to defeat Brundibar. In the end, all of them sing together in the marketplace." He looks over at Schaechter again who nods. "This is the story of *Brundibar*."

Freudenfeld sits down, and Resi says to us, "If you want to perform in *Brundibar*, stay here for more information. In a few days there will be tryouts for Aninka, Pepichek, the animals, and Brundibar. And anyone can be in the chorus, though you must agree to attend all—"

"All," Schaechter says firmly without looking up from the piano.

"Yes," Resi continues, "all rehearsals. Okay, that's it."

Everyone gets up, and within two seconds the room is somehow even noisier than it was before she first spoke.

"C'mon," Jiri says, "if we hurry we can get a game of Chinese checkers in before Apel."

"I think," I say, "I'm going to stay."

"Seriously?" Jiri says, like I've gone crazy. "Why?"

"I don't know." I shrug my shoulder, "I sort of liked the music."

"But you can't sing," Jiri says.

"Hey, how do you know?"

"Trust me, I know."

But I don't say anything, and soon Jiri's gone. So I get up and walk toward the front of the room. A few dozen kids are already gathered around Resi and Freudenfeld. Meanwhile, Schaechter remains at the piano, playing something too soft for me to hear.

July 20, 1943

"AND THEN," I SAY TO MOTHER, "THEN Otto—"

"Otto?" she asks.

"Otto *Hirsch*," I say, "I told you already."

"Oh," she says, and sits down on one of the benches in front of her barracks. She pats the spot next to her, so I sit down too. I took my dinner over to her tonight, but she insisted we eat out here. Which was a good idea, because even though the heat broke a little this afternoon, the inside of the Dresden Barracks still feels like an oven. "So, this Otto—"

"Right, he has the ball. And he's *really* good. I would pay a thousand crowns to be able to dribble like him. Seriously. All game, just like Franta said, we've been pushing them to the sideline. And it's been working, because—"

"But you were losing two to one. How is that working?"

"Because," I say, and roll my eyes, "because if we weren't doing that it would have been four to one at least by then. At least."

"You're not impressed I remembered the score?" she says, and does this thing where she tickles me behind my ear.

"C'mon, stop it."

"So then what?"

"Okay, so Otto has the ball"—I hop up off the bench—"and my job is to—"

"To force him to the sideline, yes."

"Right, but—" And for a moment I see the whole sequence in my head again, how big he is, how fast he was coming, how hard he was biting down on his bottom lip. "I know he really wants to go inside. All game he's been trying to, but we won't let him. Not me or Jiri or Leo or anyone. So guess what happens?"

"You . . ." Mother crosses her legs. "You . . . I don't know, Misha, what happened?"

"Okay, so . . ." And I start trying to show her, but it's hard all by myself. I grab her hand. "Stand up."

"Misha, please."

"C'mon."

"I'm exhausted." She pulls her hand back. "This heat, and the hours at the workshop. Plus extra time working on the set for that strange opera of yours."

"Pleeeease," I say, "it won't make sense with just me."

Mother shakes her head a few times, but then gets up. "You have fifteen seconds."

"Okay, okay. So you're Otto."

"I'm Otto?"

"And you've got the ball." But Mother just stands there. "C'mon, dribble at me."

"But I don't have a ball."

"So pretend," I say, and take a few steps back. Mother comes my way slowly, taking these small, weird steps, which I guess is her idea of dribbling. "Okay, so, if I've been pushing you to the sideline all game, and suddenly I let you go the other way, what do you do. If you're Otto?"

"I say, 'Thank you, Mr. Gruenbaum, you're so kind—'"

"I'm serious, Mother," I say, and for a second something in my throat gets stuck swallowing the words "Mr. Gruenbaum." But there's no time for that. "What do you do?"

"I go inside, right?"

"Exactly," I say, and come up close to her and turn a bit so that I'm covering her left side. "So, go."

"Go?"

"Inside!" And she starts up again with those weird steps of hers, and just like in the game, I quickly slide in front of her, all the way down to the ground, my left foot extended as far as it will go.

"Misha!" she says as she trips over my feet. She doesn't fall, but she comes pretty close, barely catching herself with one of her hands in the dirt. "Tell me something," she says, kneeling on the ground and groaning for a moment. "Have you lost your mind?"

"Sorry."

She stands back up, her face all red, wiping the dirt from her hand. "If this dress—this rag—if it rips, I'll have exactly one dress left."

"Sorry," I say, and sit back down. "Sorry." She joins me and does something with her hair.

"So after you tripped poor Otto—"

"But that's just it," I say. "I didn't trip him. It was a totally legal tackle. I stole the ball. Poked it right out from under him. He thought he had me beat, but it was me who tricked him." And I can hear it again, the way our sideline erupted, the sound Felix let out as he raced for the loose ball, Pudlina shouting his brother's name as he sprinted toward the other goal, and most of all that perfect thump as the ball shot off Felix's foot. "And just like that it was two to two."

"You scored? You didn't tell me you scored. That's wonderful, Mi—"

"No, I didn't score. Pudlina did. But I set it up. I forced the turnover."

"That's great." Mother squeezes my hand. But I can tell she doesn't really understand. Which shouldn't surprise me. She barely knows the first thing about soccer. But so what? Because it really was the turning point. Franta came up to me after the game, after Erich scored the go-ahead off a corner kick, after Koko made one last incredible save, after we all chanted "Rim, rim, rim, tempo Nesharim!" so many times so loudly I thought my throat was going to rip open, after all that Franta took me aside, put his hands on both my shoulders and said, "Misha, you little genius! I was sure you had messed up! Just ask Grizzly what I started to say. Actually, don't. I was ready to yank you out, but then, just like that, the most beautiful counterattack I've ever seen. At any level. You swung the game, Misha." He pointed at my chest. "You. If they score there, it's three to one, and I don't think we come back from such a deficit. What did I tell you? What did I say? You score one goal all season, but you manage to make the key play in the championship match!"

I turn to Mother. Her eyes are closed. "Mother?"

She jerks up straight and opens her eyes wide. "I'm sorry. Sorry. So it's two to two. You just stole the ball."

"Forget it," I say.

"No, but I want to hear."

"It's fine." I stand up from the bench. "I'll tell you tomorrow. I need to head back anyway."

"Are you sure?" she asks. "Do you have a few minutes to come inside first?"

"I really have to go. Franta—"

"I think you'll be glad you did, Misha," she says. "I have a surprise for you."

The room is quieter than I ever remember, I guess because everyone's outside where it's not so muggy. Fewer than ten women scattered here and there. "Sit down, sit down," Mother says to me when we reach her bed in one corner of the room. For some reason, she and Marietta moved spots recently.

"Hey, where's Marietta?"

"She said she was going to Hannah's room," Mother says, laughing to herself. "Those two are inseparable." Mother reaches under the bunk and pulls out a parcel maybe half the size of a shoebox.

"What's that?" I ask.

"Do you remember Max and Greta Klein?" I shake my head. "He worked with Father for a number of years." Then she stops for a moment, like she forgot what she was about to tell me.

"Yeah?" I ask.

"Max and Rose. We had them over a number of times. I know you met them." She wipes the sweat off her forehead. "Well, anyway. They're in Portugal. Her brother lives there. They were able to get out in 1940. And she sent us a package." Mother reaches her hand inside the small package and pulls out an even smaller tin.

"Sardines?" I ask. Mother nods her head and smiles. I reach my hand out to grab them.

"But wait, Misha," she says, "there's only one tin. And you know how your sister feels about them." Of course I do. Sardines were one of the top things we used to fight over back in Holesovice. And they were often part of the number one thing we'd fight over, which was the *paticka*, the crispy end of a fresh loaf of bread. Mother would bring one home, and we'd already be fighting over it before she unpacked the rest of the groceries. Of course there were two ends, but Mother wouldn't let us eat the second until the family ate its way down to it. And there's nothing better than a fat, oily sardine on the paticka. Nothing.

"Okay, okay," I say, and take the can from her. "Can I open it?"

"Of course."

I remove the small key from the top of the can, slide it into place, and begin peeling back the thin metal cover. The ends of four large sardines, two tails and two heads, come into view, their silver skin shining through the oil. My favorite, the big kind. Some kids think I'm crazy for liking sardines, but I love them too much to pretend they're gross, which I know is what most everyone else thinks.

Mother is leaning over me, watching. "Okay, so two for you, and two for Marietta." I nod my head and continue peeling. I hunch over the can, because I'm certain the other women in the room can smell what I'm smelling, that rich, fishy scent. It's probably been three years since I've actually eaten one. I expect Mother to tell me to go wash my hands or get a plate or any of the hundred things she used to tell me to do before I could eat back in Prague, but I guess the rules are different here. In fact, when I look up from the tin after opening it all the way, she's gone. I scan the room. She's at the far end, talking to Aunt Louise, who must have come down from her room on the third floor.

I lower my thumb and index finger into the tin and pull out one of the middle fish. But then I put it down, just so I can lick the oil off the tips of my fingers. Unbelievably delicious. I would drink a whole glass of it, I swear. Then I pick the sardine back up, tip my head back, and drop it in.

Somehow it's even better than I remember. I guess because it's real food. Just a fish, an actual fish. Not watery soup, not a bland slice of bread, not a mushed-up potato with no salt or butter. My throat is like a plant that hasn't been watered, a plant that's been baking in the hot sun for weeks. Because I don't chew the sardine, I just absorb it immediately. At least that's what it feels like.

I put the can down. Because now I only have one left. I need to wait, since soon I won't have any. How many could I eat? If there were a pile of these cans stacked all the way to the ceiling, how many sardines would I gobble up before I didn't want any more? A hundred? Three hundred? A thousand?

But what's the point in waiting? The can is back in my hand. I grab a sardine from along the edge. It looks a tiny bit fatter than the others, which maybe isn't fair to Marietta, but she'll never know. I try eating this one in small bites, but without a plate or a piece of bread underneath—I should have asked Mother if she had a roll hidden somewhere—it's not easy. Soon, just like that, it's gone.

Where should I leave the can? You don't just leave something this rare sitting around in a place like this. As nice as all these women look, the can would disappear in ten seconds. Mother's still talking to Aunt Louise. I could just walk over there, but Mother might not want her to see it. And there's no way I'd put it down here and go over to them without it. So I'll just wait. Mother will be back soon enough. And anyway, Aunt Louise is nice, but sometimes she pinches my cheeks, which I hate.

I wish Mother would hurry up. Because soon Franta will be mad.

Those sardines look so good. I swear they look even better than they did when I first opened the can. Like eating them reminded me of just how good they actually taste. Why can't Marietta hate them, the way she hates mustard?

Huh, that one tail is kind of bent. It's almost falling off. Which happens sometimes, I've seen it before. Sometimes they're not all identical, even if they normally are. I could just tell her the tail was missing from one. She'd believe me. Probably. And Mother was gone before I opened the can all the way. At least I think she was.

I really shouldn't. I really, really shouldn't.

But the tail is almost broken.

And I'm so, so hungry. Even after dinner and those first two sardines.

Because of what Franta said. When we got back to our room after the game, he said, "Nesharim! How I wish I had a giant cake for us all to share. A giant chocolate cake with 'Champions' written across the top in silver, no, golden, frosting." And all of us closed our eyes and pretended to eat that cake. Ever since, all I've wanted is something to celebrate with.

Why did I forget to celebrate when I ate the first two?

But it's not fair, and I shouldn't, I really shouldn't.

I really, really, *really* shouldn't.

I take the back stairway out of the barracks, because Felix told me he saw a soccer ball there yesterday afternoon. Also, that way I'll be less likely to run into Marietta, because all I can think about is the feel of that barely broken tail sliding down my throat, a tail that belonged to her. And it's true, she loves sardines even more than me.

At the bottom of the stairs I see two people in a dark, far-off doorway. They have their arms around each other, and one of them is rubbing his, or her, arms up and down the other one's back. Before I can decide if I should keep going or not, one of them walks out in the courtyard.

It's a boy, or a man, hard to tell. Maybe Franta's age, maybe younger. He's pretty tall, with broad shoulders, and he stops about ten steps from the doorway and turns around. A couple of seconds later the other person steps out, goes over to him, and takes his hand. Right before they kiss, I get a good look at the face of the second person, which wasn't really necessary to begin with, since I'd recognize Marietta skipping from twice this distance.

September 23, 1943

"MISHA," MOTHER SAYS, "HOLD THIS chair, would you? One leg is shorter than the others, I don't trust it."

"C'mon, Mother," I say, "I've got to go. There's only an hour before the show, and I need to eat dinner fir—"

"Do you want the backdrop for your opera finished or not?" she asks.

"Fine," I say, and grab the chair.

"I mean, look at that," Mother says, carefully stepping up onto it. "This house has no chimney. What kind of house has no chimney?"

It's funny, hearing Mother say something like that. It's even weirder to see her with a paintbrush in her hand. I can barely remember her ever drawing with me back in Prague, let alone doing anything artistic herself. But here it's different.

She even told me that her boss, some Dutch guy named Jo Spier, who I guess is a real artist, said she makes the best stuffed animals in the whole workshop. Her specialty is teddy bears. "How I wish I could get you one. They are rather adorable," she said a few weeks ago, which I guess was nice, so I didn't bother to tell her that I'm way too old for stuffed animals. Even so, I mentioned it to some of the guys, and they didn't believe me, didn't believe that Nazis would have us making teddy bears for them and didn't believe that Mother could make a good one.

"Mother," I say, because something suddenly pops into my head.

"Yes, dear?"

"Why don't we have to hide this the way we hide the Program? And not just this, but all the other, you know, the plays and music and everything. It doesn't make any sense."

Mother looks down at me from the chair. "I'm not sure, Misha. There's a lot about their decisions I don't understand. Why do they do any of the things they do?"

Part of me thinks she might be keeping something from me, but I don't feel like asking her again. Not right now at least.

"So, are you ready?" she asks.

"Yeah, I guess," I say. "Well, I am at least."

She doesn't ask what I mean by that last part, because she knows what I'm talking about. Rehearsals had been going great, but then, less than three weeks ago, two huge transports in one day. They were the first ones in over half a year, and just like that five thousand people disappeared, including about ten kids from the cast, along with a few Nesharim. We didn't have rehearsal for over a week, and I heard they even talked about postponing the opera completely. Eventually we started up again, but replacing the kids who left and teaching the new kids their parts hasn't been easy. And since then, I don't know, things really haven't been the same. It's like I can't ever forget that they might announce a transport at any moment. And that I might be on it. Even when I'm doing something really fun, like playing cards, I'll forget it for a moment, until I remember it again. This happens dozens of times a day, every day now.

Mother gets down from the chair, takes a few steps back, and looks up. "Well, what do you think?"

"I like it," I say. And I'm not just being polite, the backdrop really is pretty great. It actually looks like a town, with buildings, houses, a tree, even a nice round sign that says SCHOOL.

"Do you know," Mother says, "this is the hardest ticket to get in all of Terezin?"

"Seriously?"

"Oh, yes," she says, "harder than the Ghetto Swingers, harder even than that Beethoven concert last month."

And I can see Mother is about to tell me all about that again, so I say I'll see her after the show, hop off the stage, and run to dinner.

"Now remember," Mr. Freudenfeld tells us all, "slower and louder than you think you need to be. Slower *and* louder." He raises his eyebrows, which he does a lot for some reason, turning them into two upside-down V's. "How are the acoustics here in the Magdeburg Barracks?" he asks.

"They're *awful!*" all forty of us say together. He'd started saying that about these barracks a couple of weeks ago, back when we were rehearsing in the Dresden Barracks, where the sound is also pretty lousy. But I think he's right, it's actually worse here, maybe because the room is bigger. Even with just the musicians warming up nearby, I can barely hear him.

Actually only about thirty-nine of us say it, because Ela, who plays the cat, is having her makeup fixed by Mr. Zelenka, the man who picked Mother to help with the backdrop. Ela told me once that he was the most famous set designer in all of Prague before the Nazis showed up.

He even smuggled his professional makeup kit here. Her whiskers look pretty amazing.

"Good, good," Mr. Freudenfeld says, and looks at his watch. "Doors open in two minutes, and the show will start in ten." He turns and starts walking toward the musicians, but then stops and raises a finger in the air. "Oh, and one last thing. Pinta, Greta, Zdenek, Ela, Rafael, and Honza"—he smiles—"you may remove your stars for the performance."

"What?" about half the kids say. The rest, including me, are too stunned to say anything.

"We received permission"—he nods his head a bit—"for the main characters. So you may remove them."

The six of them start pulling at their stars, but only Greta gets hers off quickly. Zdenek tells Sasha to help him, and soon just about everyone has a hand on one of the five stars. Before long all of us are screaming and tearing at the horrible yellow things like they're sticky, disgusting bugs that have been crawling up and down our bodies for years.

Thirty seconds later we're all giggling fiercely, the stars on the floor, in our hands, in pieces at our feet. Their six chests look like regular chests. Like the way they must have looked before all this started four years ago, before we wound up in this horrible, ridiculous prison where they let us put on plays one day and stick us on trains to who knows where the next.

Suddenly we hear some clapping. Some of the musicians have tucked their instruments—a flute, a clarinet, and a few violins—under their arms and are giving us a standing ovation.

The room seemed impossibly big before, but now it's packed. People of every age. Kids, parents, old people—you name it. Every single chair has someone in it. We even saw a little fight, or at least a big argument, between two people over some seats by the aisle. Of course we saw it, because we're all just sitting here at the front of the room, by the side of the stage. It's not like this is a real theater or anything. There's no backstage.

Honza looks like he's going to be sick, which makes me feel like I'm going to be sick. Because Honza had the guts to play Brundibar himself, which means singing solos and being mean, all at the same time. Plus he's an orphan, in real life, and pretty tall and strong, and so this is the first time I've ever seen him look even a teeny bit worried. So it's making me very worried. And it's not just me. All the other faces—Ela, Zdenek, Greta, Pinta—they all look the same.

Mr. Freudenfeld taps a few kids on their heads. "Thirty seconds," he says.

Baby Michael in 1931

Michael's father, Karl Grünbaum, with baby Marietta, Michael's sister, 1926

Michael and Marietta Grünbaum, 1933

The Grünbaum family together

Young Michael before the war, 1936

Michael and Marietta with their father on a Sunday morning walk, circa 1938

Photo courtesy of Michael Gruenbaum

A carefree meal in the country with family and friends before the war, circa 1937

Photo courtesy of Michael Gruenbaum

Karl and Margaret Grünbaum happy together before the war

Photo courtesy of Michael Gruenbaum

Michael, Marietta, and Leci, their governess, circa 1934

Photo courtesy of Michael Gruenbaum

Aunt Louise Fleischer, Karl's sister, whose postcard helped save Michael's, Marietta's, and their mother's lives

Michael and his mother
in Prague after the war, 1946

Michael rowing a boat on the
Moldau River in Prague, 1946

Michael's mother helping him with his homework in Prague, 1945

Michael during his military service, 1954

Michael and his wife, Thelma, on their wedding day in front of their temple in Chicago, 1956

Michael and his proud mother at his MIT graduation, 1953

Michael's Czech passport photo, 1947

Michael with his surviving Nesarim "brothers" at one of their periodic reunions in Terezin

Michael and Franta Maier

Michael with his three sons, their spouses, and his grandchildren, 2014

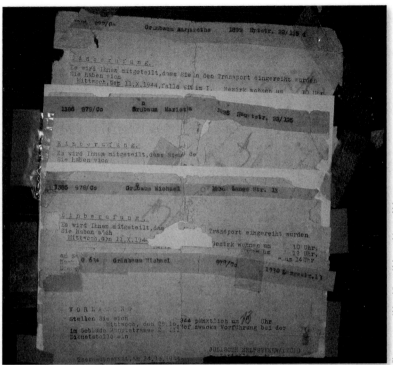

The summons to a transport from Terezin to "the east"
(Auschwitz) for the Grünbaum family

Simchat Torah card Michael made his mother in Terezin

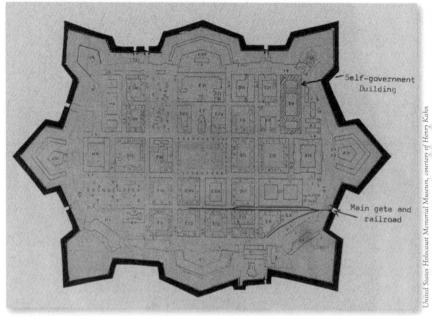

Self-government Building

Main gate and railroad

Map of Theresienstadt (Terezin)

ARBEIT MACHT FREI

Entrance to the Small Fortress at Terezin, where Michael's father was killed in 1941

Stupidly, I look back over at the audience, which includes Hans Krasa himself, the composer who wrote all the music. He came to most of our rehearsals and seemed pretty nice, but now his long face looks way too serious, like he's actually expecting this to be good. I think I even see Edelstein, the guy in charge of Terezin, at the far end of the second row.

Why didn't I listen to Jiri and go play Chinese checkers that one day?

But then something happens. We're good. We're actually good. Not great, but definitely good. Pinta and Greta really seem like brother and sister. And Ela moves like a cat. And Rafael has an amazing voice. And Honza is really, really, *really* mean. So it doesn't matter that Zdenek forgets a line or that Zvi's voice cracks.

When it's finally my turn to go up on stage with the rest of the chorus, I can't wait. All of us sing:

> *Let's extend our helping hand. . . .*
> *Add your talent to our efforts,*
> *Voice to voice, and we'll be strong. . . .*
> *United we'll win our stand.*

Singing with everyone feels a little like playing on the Nesharim team. But it's different, too. Because there's something about the story and how mean Brundibar is. We're not competing against other boys stuck here like us. We're all together fighting a really rotten person. Which is maybe why when we sing the words, we sing them like we mean it. Not to mention, when we finish the first big number, I can see it on the faces of the audience. They're happy.

We rehearsed it a bunch of times, but when we finally defeat Brundibar, when all the animals chase him off the stage, I can barely breathe I'm so excited. So excited and so happy. And something tells me I'm not the only one, because we're still in the middle of the scene, but the crowd is already clapping. So we sing over the applause:

> *We've won a victory,*
> *Battle won*
> *War is done*
> *Since we were not fearful,*
> *Since we were not tearful,*
> *Because we marched along*
> *Singing our happy song,*
> *Bright, joyful, and cheerful.*

In the middle of all this, I realize part of me is actually a little sad, because I keep remembering all those cast members who disappeared. Eva and Havel and Jan and Lev and Alena and a few whose names I never bothered to learn. They came to a rehearsal like the rest of us, not knowing it was going to be their last. Plus I still don't understand why the Nazis even let us put on this opera in the first place, an opera about fighting against an evil man with a mustache.

But that's only part of me. The rest can't stop smiling, and not just because it was fun to beat Brundibar. The truth is, it's pretty hard to be sad when the audience won't stop applauding and you have to bow for so long you're almost sick of it by the end.

November 10, 1943

"WHY DO WE HAVE TO GO TO SLEEP SO early?" Leo asks after Franta tells us to wash up. "It's barely even eight o'clock." A bunch of the other kids join in to complain, including me.

"Quiet, everyone, quiet," Franta says. After we all finally shut up, he sighs. "Listen. Tomorrow may be a very difficult day. I want everyone to be well rested."

"Difficult?" Pavel says, laughing. "What day here isn't difficult?"

"Yeah," Koko says.

"This is serious," Franta says. "There is a rumor that some-one, perhaps more than one person, has escaped, and—"

"Good for them," Pavel says.

"Pavel, please," Franta says. "Enough." Franta crosses his arms over his chest but doesn't say anything for a few seconds. "They want a full count."

"A full count of what?" I ask.

"Of everyone."

"Everyone?" Pavel asks, no longer trying to be funny.

"Yes, everyone in Terezin," Franta says.

We all burst out with a ton of questions. Everyone, as in *everyone*? Where is this going to happen, because how could they possibly find a place big enough for all of us, because we barely even fit in Terezin to begin with? When is it going to start? How long will it take? And why isn't a regular count—when they gather the count from each room in each barracks—why isn't that enough?

Franta doesn't have too many answers. In fact, he doesn't have any. So we get into bed and try to be satisfied with his promise to read to us until everyone is asleep.

I think I might already be asleep when something startles me. I look toward the door, which is open a crack, letting a sliver of light pour in. Franta stops reading. Then some loud whispering and steps coming straight at me. A few moments later Mother's standing over my bed.

"Mother? What are—"

"Take this with you tomorrow," she says, spreading the blanket, the one she's already tried to give me a couple of times, over me and Jiri.

"What are you doing?" I whisper, now definitely awake.

"It's way past curfew! They'll put you in the Small Fortress, or maybe even shoot you, if you get caught. Are you crazy?!"

"Mrs. Gruenbaum," Franta says, standing next to her. "I can't allow this."

She ignores both of us. "Take it with you. It's supposed to be cold and rainy tomorrow. Don't forget it. And dress in layers, as many as you can manage."

"Mrs. Gruenbaum," Franta says again.

Mother doesn't say anything for a few moments, just straightens out the hair near my forehead. "Franta," she finally says, very quietly. "If I see Misha out there—"

"Out where?" I ask.

"—tomorrow without this blanket, so help me God, Franta, I will . . ."

No one says anything for what seems like a long time. Not me, not Mother, not even Franta. Then she leans over, kisses the top of my head, and disappears. I look at Franta, who's rubbing his face and mumbling something I can't make out.

As soon as Mother leaves the room, I hop out of bed and run to the window. I sort of expect Franta to order me back to bed, but somehow I'm not that surprised when he appears next to me instead.

About ten seconds later, I spot Mother below, out in

front of our building. *Stay away from the lights*, I tell her in my head, and just like that she steps off the street and disappears into the darkness. She doesn't reappear, but I stay at the window anyway, following an imaginary path toward her barracks with my eyes, holding my breath, and hoping not to see any guards walking nearby.

"Okay," Franta says softly a couple of minutes later, "into bed."

But I don't move, just look up at him. He has a strange expression on his face, like he's somewhere else entirely. "Do you think . . . do you think she's okay?"

He doesn't answer for a bit. The look in his eyes only gets stranger, until he barely looks like himself at all. "Yes," he says, his voice quite dry, "yes."

November 11, 1943

IT'S DARK WHEN FRANTA WAKES US UP. I'm awake for a few seconds before I remember the thing with Mother. I assume it's just a dream until my fingers feel something weird and bring the blanket up to my eyes. I pull it over my head and try for a moment to pretend I'm back in Holesovice, in my parents' bed. But I can't pretend, even with the help of that warm, wonderful smell.

"Get up, get up," Franta says. "Your heaviest clothes, put them on. A hat, if you have one. Boots, if you have them. Hurry. We must report to the South Gate by seven a.m."

I put on three pairs of pants, four shirts, two pairs of socks, and my boots, even though one has a hole in the bottom. Then I grab my jacket and the blanket and stand by the door, waiting for everyone else.

* * *

We wait at the gate for a while, more and more people coming all the time, the sky slowly growing lighter. It starts drizzling, so a few of us try standing under a tree. But since almost all of its leaves have fallen, there's not much of a point. Then I get an idea.

"Jiri," I say, "help me up."

"Why?"

"Just do it," I say, placing the blanket on his shoulder, grabbing the trunk, and reaching toward the first big branch. Soon I'm sitting in a wide V, up above the crowd, which is still growing. I look all around, but can't find Mother or Marietta.

"Misha!" Someone's tugging at my foot. Franta. "Are you insane?! Get down from there immediately!" He helps me off, squeezing my arm so tightly it hurts. "This is not a day to stick out," he says. "Do you understand?"

"Sorry," I say, which doesn't seem to mean much to Franta right now. "I was trying to find my mother. Have you seen her?"

"What?" He raises his head a bit, and, I think, curses to himself. "No. I'll ask around." And then he definitely curses. "But it may take a while."

"How long?" I ask. But he doesn't answer.

* * *

Eventually, the gate opens and people begin streaming out through it. Still, it takes at least fifteen minutes before our part of the crowd starts moving.

I haven't seen this many SS the whole time we've been here. There must be dozens of them, each one holding a machine gun. Most every day since I've been here I've wanted to walk through these gates. But with the SS everywhere, with no one telling us where we're going or why, I'd much rather stay in bed. I'd stay there all day if I could.

But instead we march along the path we took into Terezin back when we first got here. Almost a year ago.

Maybe a half hour later, after my feet are definitely hurting and my stomach is definitely asking what happened to breakfast, the line up ahead turns off the road and into an enormous meadow.

SS officers are screaming loudly. The same thing over and over, but it takes a few minutes before our part of the line gets close enough to hear.

"Lines of one hundred! Arrange yourselves in lines of one hundred! One hundred! Exactly one hundred!"

After we get in our line, Kikina, Jiri, Leo, and I argue if the exact number means it's more or less likely that they had us come out here so they can shoot everyone. Kikina

SOMEWHERE THERE IS STILL A SUN   *229*

wants to ask Franta, but he's at least thirty people from us. In the end we can't decide, but we all agree that if we hear gunshots, we'll run away from the direction we came in, toward a grove of trees maybe a quarter mile from here.

And then we just stand there. For an hour, for two hours, for a bunch of hours. It drizzles on and off. Hour after hour.

One hundred and ninety-seven, one hundred and ninety-eight, one hundred and ninety-nine, two hundred. "Sorry, Gorila, time's up," I say. "Jiri, your turn."

"It's okay," Gorila says to me, stepping out of the blanket we were wrapped up in together. "Thanks, Misha." For a few seconds, before Jiri hurries inside, the cold, wet wind attacks me. Thank God for this blanket.

Jiri is shivering so much he can barely hold his end of it. "How long," he says, his teeth clicking against each other, "do you think we've been out here?"

"I don't know," I say. "I bet Franta does." I look down our line, one hundred people long, but don't see Franta. Which doesn't mean he's not here, because it's really hard to see past the first ten people or so. I should start counting, since Leo's next, but Jiri deserves a little extra time.

"And when," he says while his whole body shivers against mine, "are they ever going to let us go back inside?"

* * *

Kikina taps my shoulder.

"Huh?" I ask.

"Franta wants you," he says.

"Why?"

"I don't know," he says, "just go."

So I leave Jiri and Leo with the blanket and make my way toward Franta. I can't really step out of line, so I get each kid to change places with me, one at a time. Some people, like Pedro and Pudlina, give me a look like I'm trying to get us all in trouble, but after about five people I don't care one bit, because I realize there's only one reason Franta would want to talk to me right now.

"Yeah?" I say when I finally reach him, barely able to breathe.

"She's fine," he says. "She's fine."

"Really?" I say, suddenly noticing that my hands are shaking uncontrollably. He nods his head. An SS guard walks past us, his machine gun almost hitting Franta on the shoulder. Franta waits a few seconds and then picks me up.

"Look over there." He motions with his chin. I look over the lines closest to us, which until then had been blocking my view. All I can see are more lines, reaching so far that after a while they aren't separate lines at all, just people. Thousands and thousands and thousands of people.

"Where is she?" I ask.

"Over there. Seventeen, or eighteen, lines away." I try counting, but after the ninth line or so I lose count.

"How do you know?"

"I spoke to Otto Klein, and he asked Gonda Redlich to find out."

"Gonda?" I ask. "Who's Gonda?"

"You know how Otto is my boss?" Franta asks.

"Yeah."

"Well, Gonda is Otto's boss. So he knows what he's talking about. She's out there, and so is your sister. Now get down, because you might not be very big, but today at least, you're much too heavy for me."

When I get back to my spot, I wrap myself in the blanket, bend down a bit, and press my face into Jiri's back.

"What are you doing?" he asks me.

I lie and tell him, "My nose is so cold . . . I'm worried it's going to fall off." Hopefully he can't hear me sniffling.

One hundred and thirty-four, one hundred and thirty-five, one-hundred and—

"Misha," Jiri says, or maybe whispers. His voice sounds really weak. "What do you think happens if you eat grass?"

"What?" I ask, because maybe I didn't hear him right.

"If I don't eat anything soon . . . I don't know what's going—"

But then I really can't hear him, because suddenly there's a plane buzzing overhead. And not far overhead, like the planes we sometimes see way up in the sky on clear days. No, this dark gray plane is circling right over us.

A couple of lines from us, one made up of women, screaming erupts. "No! It's going to bomb us! No!" The screams grow louder. "It's going to kill us all!" A young woman with wavy, dark blond hair shrieks and starts running to the far edge of the meadow. An SS officer with a machine gun in his hands runs down the line after her. When he catches up, he pushes her hard to the ground and points his gun at her. Maybe he's saying something too, but it's hard to know, because now hundreds and hundreds of people are talking and screaming and crying.

A few minutes later she's back in line, being held up by a woman on either side. The plane continues to circle, and now it's the only sound I can hear.

"What do you think, Misha?" Jiri says. "Because cows eat grass. So maybe people can too, right?"

I know I should say something, but instead I wrap my right arm tighter around Jiri. Closing my eyes, I picture the numbers in my head, each one a different bright color: one hundred and thirty-six, one hundred and thirty-seven, one hundred and thirty-eight . . .

"How many lines do you think there are?" I ask Leo, who's just joined me under the blanket.

"How should I know?" he says.

Even with two pairs of socks on, I can feel the water soaking up through the hole in the bottom of my right boot. I try opening my mouth to catch some of the rain, because they still haven't given us anything to drink all day. Or eat either. Which is crazy, because it's starting to get pretty dark out. In fact, it sort of looks like what it looked like when we first got out here this morning, whenever that was exactly.

"And why do they keep counting us over and over? If there are a hundred people in each line, how long could it take to just add up the lines? Even if there are a ton of them. Are the Nazis that stupid?"

And just like that, an SS officer walks past, counting each one of us for the tenth time at least. "*Dreiundzwanzig, vierundzwanzig, fünfundzwanzig . . .*"

An old man collapses in the line next to ours. Two other men kneel over him for a while. Then they stand back up, leaving him on the ground. A minute after that a fourth man, tall and bald, kneels down, takes the man's jacket off and puts it on himself. A bunch of them start arguing and pointing at one another. Eventually they stop. The bald man doesn't remove the jacket.

Leo is crying. He's trying to hide it, wiping his face extremely fast every few seconds, but even though there's barely any light in the sky at this point and we're all pretty wet anyway, I can tell. And I think Erich is sleeping standing up, his shoulder leaning into mine.

"Leo, c'mon," I say, opening up the blanket.

Erich shivers and stands up straight. "What the . . . ," he says, maybe still dreaming.

Leo huddles between me and Erich. Only now we can't really close the blanket into a circle. The rain falls harder, and it's definitely getting colder. I try not to think about food. I try counting again, but I keep forgetting what number I'm on. So I let myself think about dumplings, trying to remember exactly what they taste like.

But I can't concentrate on that, either, because Leo is still crying. And maybe Erich now too.

Our line starts moving, and even though I can't feel my feet, soon I'm marching, or at least trudging slowly. Finally we're heading back. At least I hope we are.

We reach a small ridge and begin walking up it. As we

get to the top, I close my eyes for a couple of seconds, open them, and quickly look around. Before my eyes adjust I'm able to make out huge crowds of people, reaching past where I can see, in every direction.

We must be close to Terezin by now, though it's hard to tell since it's nearly pitch-black out. I can't believe I actually want to get back there, but I definitely do. Especially after I tripped over and fell onto a body at the edge of the meadow. A body that didn't respond in the slightest to my knee crashing hard right into its back.

"Hey," Jiri says, tapping on my shoulder from behind, "Franta says there were three hundred and fifty-eight lines."

I don't answer, just wrap the damp blanket around me a little tighter and keep walking.

As soon as we get back to our room, we peel off our soaking-wet clothes and lay them on the clotheslines running between the beds or just spread them flat on the floor, even though that won't do a thing. Then we put on whatever dry clothes we didn't wear today.

"Into bed," Franta says, his voice not even sounding like his.

"I'm starving," Koko says.

"We're all starving," Franta says sharply, causing Koko's face to tighten up. "I'm sorry, Koko. Please go to sleep. We'll all eat in the morning. I promise."

No one says another thing. A few minutes later the lights go out. I'm in a weird position in bed, my arm twisted under my body, but I don't have the strength to move.

"Up! Get up!" Franta is screaming. "Get up!" The light is back on; it's still night. I shut my eyes and see the meadow again. Part of me starts wondering if all that actually happened, but somehow when Franta says, "There's a fire in L414! Hurry, we must help bring water!" I know it did.

I fall out of bed, grab some pants, put on my shoes, walk around the wet clothes lying everywhere, and hurry after Franta, who is running down the hall. My limbs ache, and my throat feels like it couldn't possibly be mine. Right as we reach the door to our building, Jacob, another madrich, comes inside.

"It's out," he says.

"You sure?" Franta asks, panting.

"Yes," he says, removing his glasses and running his fingers through his thinning hair. "Go back to bed." Soon he's gone, as are the other half dozen boys who got down here before Jacob showed up. But for some reason Franta and I just stand there, not moving an inch.

Franta rubs his hands together, lowers his head, and closes his eyes.

"Why did they do that to us today?" I ask. Franta opens his eyes and starts walking toward our room. "Why?" I ask again.

"I don't know, Misha," he says. "I simply don't know." But then he stops walking, right there in the middle of the hallway.

I think I hear him take a couple of deep breaths, and then he turns to me, almost smiling, and says, "But you know what, Misha? Tomorrow's another day. And something tells me it will be a lot better than this one."

A minute later I'm back in bed, but unlike before I don't feel sleep getting any closer. My feet are still cold, the feel of that body under me at the edge of the meadow is still in my hands. I could really use that blanket right now, but I'm sure it's still sopping wet. So I turn over toward Jiri, who's already fast asleep.

Twenty minutes later, I'm still awake. In fact, I might need to pee. So I get out of bed and walk carefully toward the bathroom, trying to avoid the wet clothes everywhere.

Franta's bed is empty. Weird.

And what's that noise? Sounds like it's coming from the bathroom. Is it people talking? It's definitely coming from the bathroom, whatever it is.

I stop just outside the entrance to the bathroom, which isn't a door, just an open doorway and a sharp left turn. A bent rectangle of pretty faint light marks the entrance. The noise actually isn't very loud, but it echoes off the walls. Someone having trouble breathing.

I take a couple of soft steps and pass the very edge of the doorway. Two quick breaths and a sniffle that turns into a snort. I slowly twist my head to look.

Franta is sitting on the ground, his back pressed against the wall and his head down. I can make him out pretty well, because some pale yellow light, coming through a window I can't see, is landing right on him. His broad shoulders shake for a few seconds and then stop. He slowly raises his head and the light reflects off all this wetness on his cheeks.

"What . . ." I think he says, but he says it so quietly. I lean in just a bit more and hold my breath. "What . . ." He says it again, I'm sure this time, but then he stops, maybe because of his crying and sniffling. I really need to breathe, but something tells me he's not done talking yet, even though I don't understand why he's talking, since he's all by himself. I grab the doorframe and lean in a bit more. He slowly shakes his head back and forth. "What about tomorrow?" he says. Then he uses the back of his left hand to wipe his face, which only changes the reflection.

I stand up straight, turn around, take a long, deep breath, and head back to bed.

On my way there I stop at the tiny furnace by the door. The thing is supposed to heat our room, but it couldn't heat a space a tenth this size. Still, Franta let me put the blanket on the part of floor closest to it. I lean down and grab the corner by the furnace. The very tip of it is actually dry.

Without thinking about it, I get all the way down on my hands and my knees and bring my nose to the dry part. I breathe in and out a few times before figuring out what it is I'm smelling. Not Holesovice. Just that meadow, cold and wet.

December 17, 1943

"WELL," DR. LAMM SAYS, "THE RASH IS finally gone and you're still peeling." He lifts my arm up and rubs the skin near my armpit. A tiny shower of flaky skin falls to the floor. I put my arm down quickly, not wanting any of the other thirty kids here to see, but no one even seems to notice. "That's a good sign."

"Can I go then?" I ask, wishing that they'd at least let me get back into bed. This cement floor feels like rough ice.

He doesn't answer, just puts his cold hand up by my throat and presses, which hurts a little. "Greta," he says to the short nurse, "feel this." So she puts her hand, much warmer than his, in the same spot.

"Still swollen," she says.

"So I can't?" I ask. But he ignores me. For some reason

he's not very friendly today, like it's my fault I got scarlet fever in the first place.

"Stick out your tongue, Misha." I do as he says. "Hmm. What was his temperature this morning?"

Greta looks at the small pad of paper she carries around everywhere. "Uh . . . one hundred point two. Down from yesterday." He looks over at the pad and nods his head.

"Okay," he says, "back into bed with you." I cover myself up with the itchy blanket and touch my throat, wondering what they were checking for there. "Once your temperature gets below ninety-nine, you may return to your room. And that might be as soon as Sunday."

"Two more days?" I ask, and punch the mushy mattress. "C'mon, I've been here eleven days already."

But Dr. Lamm is already at the next bed, where some Dutch girl I can't even talk to has been for the last few days. She's asleep, so Dr. Lamm and Greta just stand at the foot of her bed, talking quietly. I have a hunch they're not talking about her, because I keep hearing them mention other people's names. Greta shakes her head and stares at the floor. There's something about the expression on her face I really don't like, so I look out the window on the other side of my bed, even though there's nothing to see out there, just the gray barracks and the tips of a couple of naked trees.

I'm so bored I pick up the pad of paper Mother brought me earlier in the week, even though the only thing I've done with it is write her one letter. The pen I used barely worked at all, so I had to press extra hard. If I hold the pad up to the light just right, I can still read what I wrote on the page that used to be under the one I actually wrote on:

Dear Mother:

There is a doctor here who once sent me to have my appendix taken out (when I was three I think). There is also a nurse here whose name is Schultz and who knows you. I ate up all the bread, but I can't make toast here. I am <u>very hungry</u>. The doctor says I'm peeling. What did he tell you? Why doesn't anyone from Room 7 write to me? Leo Lowy says to send regards to Honza Deutsch. What's new with Jiri, Kikina, and Felix? Maybe they can all come with you and Marietta next time you visit. I can't wait to see you.

   Misha

"I'm so bored," I tell Greta about an hour later with the thermometer in my mouth. "Why can't I go back to my room?"

Greta doesn't say anything. She reaches out and removes the thermometer. "One hundred point one," she says to herself and jots it down in her pad.

"I'm serious," I say.

She looks at me like she had forgotten I was here. "Why don't you read your memory book?"

"Again?"

"And why not?"

"Because I've only had it for a couple of days, and I've already memorized the whole thing."

"Well," she says, sticking her pen behind her ear, "if my friends bothered to make me something like that, something to remember them by . . ." She blinks quickly a few times.

"Yeah?"

"I'd cherish it." She swallows and smiles a weird, fake smile. "I would." She bends over and picks the notebook up from the floor under my bed. "'*Memory Book of Michael Gruenbaum,*'" she reads aloud, admiring the cover, "'Terezin, December 1943.' They thought of you while you were gone. That boy, what's his name?"

"Jiri," I say, annoyed, taking the thing from her.

"He even delivered it himself. Such a sweet boy."

After she leaves to talk with some younger boy a few beds from me who keeps moaning, I start leafing through the book again. In small, tight letters:

When you open this memory book one day and
reminisce about the time we spent in Terezin,
think of me too. Your friend Robin Herz.

In tall, slanting letters:

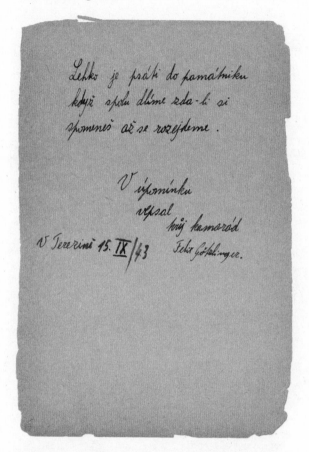

It is easy to write in a memory book when
we live together, but will you still remember
me when we're apart? In memory, your pal,
Felix Gotzlinger.

Near the end, in tiny, block letters:

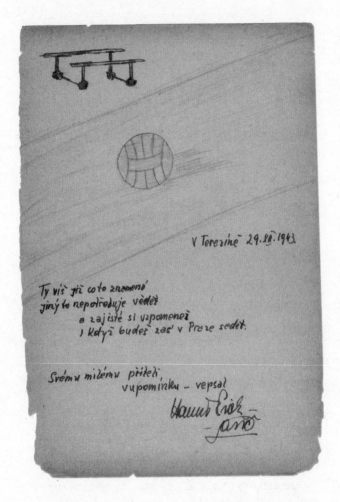

*You know what this means, nobody else has
to know, and you'll definitely remember, even
when you're sitting in Prague again. To my
close friend, in memory, Hanus Pick.*

And a drawing of a soccer ball. I'll have to ask him what he's talking about, because I actually have no idea. I close the book and my eyes, then open it to a random page. In thin, curving letters below the drawing of an eagle:

> *Someday we'll be back home in Prague,*
> *talking about the Nesharim and all our*
> *victories. And we'll still be best friends then,*
> *right? In memory, your pal, Jiri Roth.*

I set the book down on my lap and stare out the window. It was pretty nice for him to deliver it. And the funny thing is they must have started putting it together before I asked Mother why none of the Nesharim were writing to me, because Jiri brought it by only a couple of hours after someone delivered my letter to her.

I guess I'm not that much better yet, because I slept for half the morning but still feel like I need to rest again.

Some time later—I must have been sleeping—some other woman walks in and hugs Greta. They talk for a while by the door. Then they hug again. Both are crying. The woman leaves and Greta sits down on a chair, wiping her face with the bottom of her palm. When she gets up and walks toward my bed, I pretend I'm asleep.

Tap . . . tap . . . tap.

Was I asleep again? And where's that noise coming from?

Tap . . . tap.

The window. I let the memory book drop from my chest onto the floor. Then I get up and walk over to the window. *Tap*, louder this time. A small stone, a pebble probably, knocking against the window.

I look out. Jiri's down below. Three stories below. He waves. So I wave back. He says something, or at least I think he does, because I can see his mouth open, and his breath comes out like a little cloud. But I can't hear what he says. I hold my hands up to my side and shake my head back and forth. He does this thing with his arms, almost like he's running in place, his fists making circles by his sides. I shrug my shoulders. He points to his right, then at himself, then out to the right again. Then he does that thing with his arms again and smiles, though it doesn't look like a very happy smile. I wave and rest my hand against the window, which is freezing.

He stands there for a while, just staring up at me. Then he waves, turns around, and walks away.

I stay at the window until he disappears around the corner of the building. Still trying to figure out what that was all about, I get back in bed. Suddenly I realize he was wearing a backpack over one of his shoulders. I jump out of bed and run to the door. I'm about halfway there when Greta grabs my arm.

"What are you doing?"

"Let me go!" I shout, and try tearing her hand away, which is much stronger than makes any sense.

"Misha, stop, you can't—" But I finally rip her hand off and run out the door. But as soon as I turn left toward the stairs, I bump right into Dr. Lamm, who accidentally knocks me to the ground.

"Misha?" he says as Greta's footsteps get closer. I hop up and try to keep going, but four hands are too many for me to escape from.

"Leave me alone!" I scream.

"Calm down," Dr. Lamm orders. Only I can't, because I don't want to. I feel myself thrashing back and forth, and for a split second notice a half dozen kids staring at me from the doorway. Greta puts her arms around me and hugs me so tight I can't move at all. I want to break free, but my whole body feels so weak I'm scared it's going to fall apart.

"Shh . . . shh," Greta says, rubbing my back. "It's okay, Misha, it's okay." And even though I want to push her away and go find Jiri, I let her hold me like that for a while, until I can tell that the kids and even Dr. Lamm are gone. "It's okay, it's okay."

"Is there . . . ," I start to say a while later, but I still can't catch my breath.

"Is there what?" Greta asks.

"A transport," I say to her shoulder. "There is, isn't there?"

"Yes," she says into the top of my head after a long pause. "There is."

It had to be Jiri's idea to have them make me the book while I was stuck here. But I didn't get to ask him, because when he delivered it a couple of days ago, they wouldn't even let him past the doorway. So we just waved to each other back then, too. Still, I'm positive it was his idea.

> Someday we'll be back home in Prague,
> talking about the Nesharim and all our
> victories. And we'll still be best friends then,
> right? In memory, your pal, Jiri Roth.

I turn the book back to the beginning, because suddenly I feel like reading through the whole thing again, from start to finish. And there on the first page, which is Koko's page:

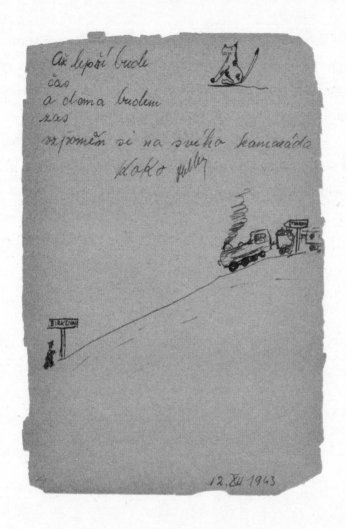

As soon as times are better and we're home,
remember your pal Koko Heller.

Below his drawing of a dog he drew a train, with smoke swirling out of the front. It's passing a sign that says

TEREZIN and is heading straight downhill toward another sign. That one says BIRKENAU, that other name for the East. It better not be so bad there, though right now it's hard to convince myself it's anything but.

I close the book very carefully and stare out the window, trying to remember what those taps sounded like, wishing they'd start up again.

May 31, 1944

"C'MON, TOMMY, PUSH!" I SCREAM FROM
my corner of the wagon.

"I can't," he says. "It's stuck. Look."

So I walk over to his end to see. The back wheel has
fallen a few inches into a crack in the street.

"Maybe if we were coming back from the Dresden Barracks," Tommy says, "and this thing wasn't weighed down
with all these loaves, maybe then we could lift it."

"Well," I say, winking, "what if a few, you know,
fall out?"

Tommy's eyes grow wide. "Misha!" he whispers loudly,
"a few rolls is one thing, but actual loaves of bread?"

He's right. That wouldn't be the best idea. Because
you can hide rolls, especially when your pants, even
though you've had them for four years, are as loose as

mine. But hiding a loaf of bread is another story. Too bad, because yesterday I traded a couple of rolls with a woman for the end of a salami. This is definitely the best job in the whole camp, even if we barely understand anything the Danish men who run the bakery say to us. Plus, Tommy's really nice and even listens to me, probably because I'm older and officially in charge of our wagon. We get to walk all over Terezin, and a lot of the time we get to choose the route. Also, I was able to get Kikina a job here too, and he won't stop thanking me for that. Oh, and of course, working for the bakery gets me out of classes. Maybe it's not so good to be missing so many lessons, but I'll take being full and stupid over smart and hungry any day.

"What if we rock it back and forth?" I say to Tommy. "Maybe that'll work."

We try that for a while, only the thing won't budge, probably because it's as long as me and Tommy put end to end. Eventually a man with a mustache and thick stubble walks by, so we ask him for help.

"You two grab that end, and I'll push from here," he says from my corner and puts his unbelievably dirty hands near the bottom of the wagon. It takes a while, but after rocking it back and forth about twenty times, we finally lift it up and out.

"Thanks a bunch, mister," I say after we've got it rolling again.

"No problem," the man says, walking alongside the wagon, like he's just taking a leisurely stroll with us. We turn a corner and go down a narrow street between two large buildings. "Hey," the man says quietly, looking behind us, "how about, uh, something for my troubles?"

"Huh?" I ask.

He points at the wagon with his thumb. "Awful lot of bread there. I can't imagine anyone would notice one less loaf."

I stop pushing and look at Tommy, who stops pushing too. But he just raises one of his shoulders and murmurs something I can't hear. So I reach into my pants and pull out a yeast roll.

"They count the loaves," I say, handing it to the man. "And this tastes better anyway."

The man quickly grabs the roll and takes a huge bite.

"Hey, mister," Tommy says, "why are your hands so dirty?"

"Tommy," I whisper, shaking my head.

"What?" he says back, because I guess he has no idea you shouldn't say stuff like that, especially to adults.

"Been planting flowers all week," the man says, taking another bite, "getting our little paradise ready for some esteemed visitors."

"Visitors?" I ask. "What visitors?"

"Not sure exactly. I hear it's got something to do with the Red Cross," he says, talking with his mouth full. "All I know for sure, they're not painting the barracks and building you kids a playground and installing benches everywhere just because they suddenly decided they like us Jews after all. The only thing they do for us is tell us which train to get on." He laughs quickly and then cuts himself off. "Seven thousand five hundred people in four days, and the day after that they're planting grass everywhere, like this is some kind of vacation getaway." He sticks his finger into his mouth, picks something off his back teeth, and then makes a sucking sound. "Okay, back to landscaping detail," he says, and starts walking toward where we first met him. "Thanks for the snack, gentlemen."

After work and the longest Apel ever (Franta made us hunt for bedbugs, which have been pretty awful lately), I go to the Dresden Barracks. I was able to schlojs half a loaf at the end of work, stuffing a quarter in each pocket, and I want to give them to Mother and Marietta.

Their room is pretty empty. Which isn't surprising, because I sort of wondered if anyone would be here at all. When I left our building, I noticed a ton of people in the town square, where they never even used to let us go. But they took down the giant tent, and now some orchestra plays there in the evening under the new wooden pavilion the Nazis had us build. And if people don't like what they're playing, they can go to the coffeehouse across the street and hear the Ghetto Swingers play jazz instead. The other day I even saw a man play the trombone, which must be the most amazing instrument ever.

It's like if you weren't really paying attention, you might think this isn't just a massive prison.

Marietta is sitting at a table, reading a book. I don't see Mother anywhere.

I walk quietly over to my sister but don't say hi, just place the bread over what she's reading.

"Hey," she says, annoyed, before she notices what's blocking her view and who brought it. "Misha Gruenbaum," she says, admiring the bread, "master schlojser."

"You're welcome," I say. But she doesn't say anything, just keeps looking at the bread. "Go ahead, it's yours. I have another chunk just like that for Mother." Marietta carefully tears off part of the crust and takes a bite. "Hey, where is she, anyway?"

"In bed, I think," Marietta says, motioning with her head, since she's already reading again. "Something"—she lowers her voice—"is bugging her. But she won't tell me what."

Mother is in bed, but I missed her, maybe because she's curled up like a tiny ball.

"Hi," I say. She tries to smile at me, but it doesn't really work. "I brought you some bread. From work."

"Thanks," she says softly. "But I'm not hungry. You should have it."

"No, it's for you," I say, placing the bread on the thin edge of the bed frame. "I'll get more tomorrow."

She doesn't say anything. Instead she lifts up one of her arms. "Come," she says. I'm not that interested in joining her, since I know some of the guys were going to play soccer, only she looks so sad. She rolls over a bit, revealing a postcard she was lying on for some reason. I reach out for it, but she snatches it before I can.

"Who'd you get a postcard from?" I ask.

"It's nothing," she says.

"Nothing?" But she doesn't answer. So I grab it out of her hands.

"Misha!" she says, trying to get it from me, but I'm already a few steps away from her bed. Only the postcard doesn't really say much.

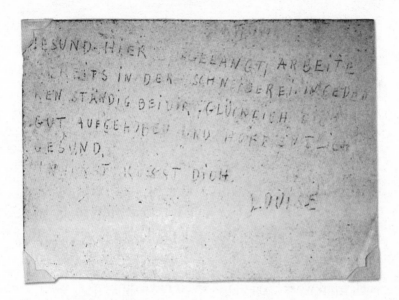

We arrived here in good health and I am
already working as a seamstress. Best regards
and wishes for good health.

It's from Aunt Louise, who left on one of the transports with Uncle Ota about two weeks ago. The return
address says, "Birkenau." Other than Mother's name and
the address here, that's pretty much it.

"What's the big deal?" I say. "It barely even says anything." Mother gets up and takes it from me, but still
doesn't answer. "I don't see why you're in such a bad
mood. She said everything's fine. Plus the weather is
finally warm here and this place isn't so ugly anymore.
Not to mention the air raid yesterday, right? Franta

said they were Allied planes. And if they're flying over Terezin, how far could they be from Germany? I bet we'll be back in Prague in a couple of weeks. You'll get to see Aunt Louise then."

Marietta walks over and pulls the postcard out of Mother's hand. "Why didn't you show me this?" she asks quickly.

"It's nothing," Mother says, lying back down.

"Right," Marietta says, "and I'm sure this nothing has nothing to do with why you've been in bed since you came back from work. You didn't even have dinner."

I look back and forth from Marietta to Mother, trying to figure out what's going on. But Marietta's just standing there with her arms crossed, while Mother stares at the bottom of the bunk above her.

"Do you see," Mother finally says, almost in a whisper, "do you see how the handwriting slants down like that?"

I look at the postcard, the writing is definitely slanting down.

"Yeah, so?" Marietta says.

"We made an agreement. Louise and I. Before she left."

"What do you mean, agreement?" I ask.

"We knew they'd make them send something like this, so . . ." Marietta has the strip of crust near her mouth but isn't actually eating it. "If things are good there, she'd write slanting up. Slanting down means things are bad."

"Bad how, Mother?" Marietta asks. She doesn't get an answer.

"Maybe she got mixed up," I say. "Maybe she thought slanting down means good. Anyhow, it says she got a job already. Right? Because how bad can being a seamstress be?" I look over at Marietta for support, but she's watching Mother and doesn't seem too convinced by my reasoning. "She arrived in good health. It says so."

"Bad how?" Marietta tries again.

"Or maybe it's just a little worse," I say. "Like, I don't know, maybe there aren't any good musicians there. That's possible, right?"

"Anyway," Marietta says, "Gustav told me things will be pretty much the same there." Mother shakes her head slightly and maybe laughs. "What?" Marietta says, sounding insulted. "What makes you so sure he's wrong?"

"Who's Gustav?" I ask. No one answers me. "Who is he?"

"My boyfriend," Marietta finally says.

"Is he tall?" The words come out before I realize it.

Marietta makes a weird face. "What?"

"Nothing," I say.

"Um, well, yes, he's kind of tall. But why does that matter?"

"He says it's okay there?" I ask.

Marietta nods.

"He's just a boy," Mother says. "How could he possibly—"

"Seventeen isn't a boy, Mother," Marietta says angrily. "He knows what he's talking about. And anyway, they haven't put us on a transport yet, so we don't have to worry."

Mother picks up the bread, takes a bite, and chews slowly. "Actually, they did put us on a transport—"

"What?" I ask. Marietta crosses her arms again.

"But I was able to speak with someone on the Council. I reminded them of what Father did for the community back in Prague. They agreed to remove us."

"When was this?" Marietta asks.

"A couple of weeks ago." Mother picks up the post-card and sticks it in a thin space between the mattress and the bed frame. "And they . . . they put . . . they put Misha on one a few days later, but I was able to do the same."

"Just me?" I ask. "Why just me?"

But Mother doesn't respond, just curls back into the shape of a ball. I almost ask my question again, but in the end I don't. Instead I just say bye, or maybe I don't, and hurry out, trying hard to think about nothing but soccer.

June 23, 1944

"NOW WHAT ARE YOU GOING TO SAY WHEN you receive the cans?" some Jewish man, who keeps touching a sore on his cheek, asks all of us while we're waiting for the visitors to arrive.

"Sardines again, Uncle Rahm?" the line of us says.

"Louder," he tells us. "You're sick of eating sardines, *every single day*. Right? Now try again."

"Sardines *agaaaiiin*, Uncle Rahm?" we say.

"Good, good," he says, not looking all that pleased. "Much better."

"I don't want sardines; I *hate* sardines!" Pavel says and stomps his feet, like he's about to have a tantrum. Then he cracks up.

The man walks over to him. "You think this is funny?"

"Not if I actually get some sardines," Pavel says with a big smile on his face.

"You think Commandant Rahm has a sense of humor?" Pavel doesn't say anything. "Do you?" Pavel shrugs his shoulders and grins. The man touches the spot on his cheek, maybe picking at something there. Suddenly he smacks Pavel, so hard Pavel nearly falls over. For a few seconds no one does anything, until Pavel spits at the man's feet. The man tries to smack him again, but Pavel ducks. "Get out of here, now!" the man shouts. "Or you'll be sleeping in the Small Fortress tonight. Don't think I can't arrange it."

The Small Fortress. Where they sent Father. Just hearing it makes my skin crawl. I still don't know exactly what goes on there. All I do know, I've never heard of anyone coming *back* from there.

Pavel jogs off. "Say hi to Uncle Rahm for me," he says to Felix and me as he passes by.

Just then four shiny black cars pull up. The first one stops, and the driver, a stocky SS officer, gets out, walks to the back and opens the door. A Jew in a dark, fancy suit gets out.

"A Jew with a chauffer?" I whisper to Felix.

"That's Eppstein," he whispers back.

"Eppstein?"

"Franta said he replaced Edelstein, the guy who used to be in charge."

"What happened to Edelstein?"

"No idea," Felix says.

Someone shushes us just as I was about to ask Felix if he thinks Eppstein has a black eye or not. Because I'm pretty sure he does. Men in suits get out of the other cars, along with one other SS officer, from the last car.

The second SS officer, who has a high forehead and his hair shaved on the sides, walks to the far end of our line, which has maybe forty kids in it. The man who had us rehearse what to say is standing there very straight, holding a cardboard box in his hands. The SS officer walks over to him, reaches his hand into the box and pulls out a small stack of tin cans.

"Sardines!" the man with the box says, like he's surprised or something. He looks at us with his eyebrows raised.

"Sardines again, Uncle Rahm?" we say, almost in unison. The rest of the adults, who must be from the Red Cross, stand together by the cars. A couple whisper to each other. One stands with his arms crossed. Another writes something down in a small notebook. Will they really believe this whole thing? That Rahm gives us sardines? That we'd complain to him? Could they be that stupid?

And are there really sardines inside these cans?

A minute later, Rahm, who smells like too much after-shave, places a can into my outstretched hand. I say thank you, but he doesn't say you're welcome.

"Who cares that we didn't get to keep the sardines," I say to Kikina, "so long as we're getting a lunch like this." I look down at my dull metal plate, which has about three times as much food on it as normal. Plus it's real food. Mashed potatoes, onions, cucumber salad, and tongue.

"Too bad the Red Cross doesn't visit every day," Shpulka says, cramming a forkful of mashed potatoes into his mouth.

"I don't know," Kikina says. "I don't think I could clean our room for that long ever again. That was way too much, even for Franta."

"Do you think they'll actually buy it?" I ask.

"Buy what?" Shpulka asks.

"I don't know," I say. "Everything. This lunch, and those flowers, and just how great everything looks here now."

"Why wouldn't they?" Kikina asks. "How would they know the difference?"

"Well," I say, "they'd find out pretty quick if they actually asked anyone."

"And do you think the Nazis are going to let *that* happen?" Shpulka says. "Yeah, right."

We eat for a while longer, no one saying anything. This food tastes pretty amazing, but the whole thing with the Red Cross makes my stomach feel a little weird at the same time.

"Hey," Shpulka says, "who are the teachers playing today?"

"The electricians," Kikina says.

"Of course," Shpulka says, shaking his head, "the two best teams. So the Red Cross can see how great the soccer is here in lovely Theresienstadt."

Kikina sticks his tongue out, which has some tongue on it. We all laugh.

"When's the game?" I ask.

"I think around four," Shpulka says.

"Oh man," I say, "I've got to do *Brundibar* then."

"Have fun," Kikina says.

"Do you think that those Red Cross people, do you think they'll get what the opera is really about?" I ask.

"I doubt it," Kikina says. "If they were smart enough to figure that out, they'd know that this whole visit is a joke, and it wouldn't matter."

"But so why are they here in the first place?" I ask. Only no one answers. My food is slowly starting to taste better and worse at the same time for some reason. "And wait, do you think . . . do you think maybe this is why they let us do plays and operas in the first place? Even though we can't have school—"

"But we do have school," Shpulka says.

"No we don't," I answer back quickly.

"Didn't you hear?" he says. "They turned a couple of rooms into a school, only—"

"Where?" I ask.

"I don't know," Shpulka says, "over by the Hamburg Barracks, I think."

"You're lying," Kikina says.

"If you'd let me finish," Shpulka says, "you'd know I wasn't. My father told me himself. They made a few rooms look like classrooms. But then, get this, they put a sign on the entrance. It says"—Shpulka sticks his hand out in front of us and moves it from one side to the other—"'School Closed for Vacation.'"

The three of us laugh, even though I'm not sure it's all that funny.

"But wait," I say. "Seriously, maybe that's why they let us put on operas and play music and everything. Even though we can't actually have school. So they can show us off. Right? Maybe that's why. So people will think the Nazis actually care about us."

"Yeah," Shpulka says, "and next week they're starting to film a movie here to show the whole world how great this place is."

"They are?" I ask.

"I was kidding," Shpulka says.

"Oh," I say, even though I wouldn't be surprised if he told me he wasn't kidding after all.

No one says anything else, we just go back to chewing our delicious food, at the edge of a sidewalk that got cleaned so thoroughly on Wednesday that we've been forbidden to walk on it ever since.

Today's *Brundibar* performance, which is at least our twentieth by now, is better than usual. Maybe because they have us perform in the Sokol Building, which I guess is now supposed to be called the Community Center, in a huge room that actually has a balcony.

I can't tell if or when the Red Cross visitors come. All I know is that we sing extra loud today, especially at the end. Like maybe they'll somehow get the message then and make the Nazis shut down Terezin and send us all back home. Of course, after we finish and the applause ends, nothing else happens. It's just like any other performance. Still, I'm a little excited. Because as soon as Freudenfeld, the director, says it's okay, I take off for the bashta, hoping to catch the end of the game between Franta's team and the electricians.

I race through the camp, past the new playground, past the packed pavilion, where the orchestra is warming up, past the neat rows of blue and pink and orange flowers, past wide stretches of actual green grass. The buildings are almost sparkling, they're so clean. I get to the edge of the bashta and quickly run up the stairs. Only when I get to the top do I realize that someone's built a railing along them.

There's maybe twenty, twenty-five people up here, none of them much older than me. Darn, I missed the game. I notice Pedro and Zdenek Taussig from Room 1 and run over to them.

"Is it over?" I ask.

"Wow," Zdenek says. "What a match."

"What do you mean? What happened?"

"Teachers won, three to two," Pedro says. "Franta was amazing. You should have seen it. A couple of times he jumped straight out to the side. I swear, he was completely parallel to the ground! And still he was able to catch the ball, or at least punch it away. He's not scared of anything. I bet he'll play pro someday."

A few minutes later we've got our own match going. Everyone seems to be in a pretty good mood, even Zdenek and the rest of the kids from Room 1. We play for around an hour and only stop because Apel is coming up.

"If it was like this all the time," Pudlina says, kicking the ball ahead as we head back to L417, "I wouldn't mind staying here. I wouldn't."

"But what if staying here still means transports sometimes?" I ask.

"It doesn't matter," Hanus says, kicking the ball away from Pudlina, "because the Americans are already in France. We'll be back in Prague in no time."

"Speak for yourself," Erich says. "I'm going back to Brno. Prague is stupid. I mean, how can a city that big have such lousy teams?"

"What are you talking about?" I say, but no one seems to care, since the rest of the guys are all fighting over the ball about ten feet from me. I decide to get in there myself, so I hurry over and kick the ball extra hard just as it squirts out toward me. It flies into the air, bounces off a tree, and sails over a brick wall.

"Way to go, Misha," Pudlina says. "Now go get it."

"Isn't that the Vrchlabi Barracks?" Kikina asks.

"I think so," Hanus says. Kikina shakes his head and shivers a bit.

"What?" I ask. "What does that mean?"

"C'mon, go get it," Pudlina says. "Apel starts soon."

I want to say no, but I guess it was my fault. And this

is the best ball we've had in months. "Okay," I say, "but someone's going to need to help me over the wall."

A minute later Felix and Erich are holding the bottom of my shoes and complaining that I weigh a ton. "Just a bit higher," I tell them. Finally I reach the top of the wall and pull myself up. It actually feels good in my arms to pull like this. Maybe the tongue gave me extra strength or something.

I drop down as a bad, sour smell hits me. Then I look up. I'm inside a courtyard I've never been in before. Lying everywhere on stained sheets, or just on the dry, dirty ground, are sick people, most of them very old, all of them incredibly thin. I don't know if it's some weird light or something, but they all look kind of yellow, except for the red spots and rashes all over their bodies. The ball is just sitting there, resting between two of them, but they don't even seem to notice.

For a few seconds I think about telling everyone I couldn't find it. But instead I walk over. The smell, which is pee and something much worse than pee, grows stronger with each step. I hold my breath and pick up the ball. Even though I'm trying to look away, I accidentally make eye contact with an old man. His eyes are both silver or gray, and I sort of get the feeling he doesn't actually see me. His teeth are so yellow they're nearly brown.

"Bruno?" he says.

I stand there for a few seconds, trying to figure out what happened to his eyes.

"Bruno? Is that you?"

But I don't answer him, just kick the ball back over. Then I grab a rickety wooden chair resting on its side in the middle of nowhere, bring it up to the wall, and hurry to the other side.

"Hey," I say a minute later, "do you think the Red Cross is still here?"

"Nah," Kikina says, "my older brother told me they already left. Why?"

But I don't say anything, and no one seems to notice that I'm walking so slowly that I fall way behind the rest of the group. As L417 comes into view I hear the orchestra start up again, playing something familiar. I guess I must have heard it once or twice on our radio back home, when we'd sit in the living room after dinner, my parents drinking tea and me asking for just one more cookie.

September 24, 1944

THE MOMENT I HEAR THE RUMOR, I TELL Tommy we need to go, now. Sure it was just two random women on the street, but I'm not taking any chances.

"But what about the last delivery?" he asks.

"It can wait," I tell him.

We quickly push the wagon back to the bakery, almost running over a few people in the process. Then we just leave the thing there, not caring that it's a third full of rolls for the Hannover Barracks, one of the men's barracks. Because if those women are right, then that's a pointless delivery to begin with.

Tommy and I sprint—and I mean sprint—across the ghetto. And I can see on the faces of at least half the people we pass that the rumor is spreading fast. It's been over five months since the last big one, which somehow only makes it worse.

* * *

I stumble into our room. Franta's at one of the tables, and about half the guys have already arrived, every one of them no more than ten feet from him.

"Is it true?" I say, completely out of breath.

No one answers right away, but I can tell it is. Because most of the kids are crying, and no one's really doing anything else. No games are being played, no books are being read. No one's even talking. They're all just frozen, especially their faces. Except Kikina, who's steadily punching the table with the side of his fist.

And then there's Franta, who sort of looks like he's having a conversation with himself. His eyes are darting around, his forehead wrinkling and unwrinkling and wrinkling up again. His chest expands as he takes a deep breath. Then he holds it for a few seconds, closes his eyes and exhales.

"Is it?" I ask again, squeezing in between Felix and Leo at the table.

Hanus nods.

"When?"

"Tomorrow," Shpulka says, "starting tomorrow."

"It may take a bit," Franta finally speaks. "Five thousand people can't go out in just one day."

"Five thousand?"

"All men, sixteen to fifty-five," Hanus says. "All of them."

"Supposedly they're going to start a new labor camp somewhere," Shpulka says.

So that explains why the room isn't more full. Because pretty much all the fathers must be going. Pavel's, Erich's, Koko's, and a bunch of others—all are going. Then they'll be like me. Well, sort of anyway.

"Don't go." The words come out of my mouth before I realize I'm saying them. "You can't." Somehow this starts Kikina crying.

"I have no choice," Franta says. "I'm not a protected person, I—"

"What about Gonda?" I say. "Your boss's boss. He'll get you off the list. For sure he will. I mean, c'mon, you're the best madrich here."

Franta smiles. "Well, if Gonda weren't going himself, perhaps I could."

Usually when I cry, which isn't that much, I feel it coming. Which lets me fight it. Mostly I win. Even when I don't, at least I have time to prepare, to go off somewhere so I can do it alone. Only now it just happens all at once. Franta gets blurry, and I feel like I need to blow my nose. But I don't care. When everyone's crying, what does it matter?

The door opens, and Pavel comes in, biting his bottom lip.

"How are they doing?" Franta asks him. Pavel just shrugs his shoulders.

"Wait," I say, "what about our room? Who's going to live with us now?" All the heads not already facing Franta turn to him.

"They're evacuating L417—"

"What?"

"Why?"

"They can't just—"

"Most of you," Franta continues, sounding like he's telling us nothing more than the time of the afternoon Apel, "will live with your mothers. There is talk of setting up another children's barracks."

"But what about the Program?" Erich asks.

"Those remaining will do their best to continue it," Franta says.

"No!" Kikina says. "It's not fair. It's not." Suddenly he stands up, grabs the ladder leading up to one of the bunks, and starts shaking it. When that doesn't do anything, he starts kicking it. I watch for a couple of seconds, but eventually turn away around the time the wood cracks.

"Kikina," Franta says firmly, "enough." A couple of kicks later Kikina stops and collapses onto one of the beds. Franta stands up and walks over to his own bed. He pulls a small suitcase out from under the bunk, places it on his bed, and begins packing. From the sound of it, I can tell that everyone who wasn't crying before is now. For a moment, Franta pauses, the muscles in his jaws sticking out. After a few seconds of doing nothing, he slams his suitcase shut and comes back to the table. But he doesn't sit down.

"Shpulka," he says.

"Huh?"

"What are the rules here?" Shpulka doesn't respond. "In our room, Shpulka, what are the rules?"

Shpulka sniffles and wipes his nose with his sleeve. "Make your bed, every morning."

"What else?"

"Check for bedbugs."

Franta nods.

"And . . . and keep the bathrooms clean. Someone has to do that."

"Good," Franta says, "what else? Someone other than Shpulka."

"And yourself," I say. "You have to keep yourself clean."

"Is that all?" Franta asks, almost smiling. "Are the Nesharim merely hygiene experts?" We look around at one another the way we do when some ex-professor asks us a tough question about history, or science. "Nothing? That's it?"

"Be nice," Felix says. "To everyone."

"And share," Pedro says, "even when it's hard."

"Be on time," Kikina says straight into the mattress, without even lifting his head up. A few of us laugh.

"Work together," Kapr says.

"No names," Felix says, "no calling people names."

Franta's nodding. "You see," he says, "you don't need me, you already know—"

"And stick together," I say. "But this isn't sticking together." I feel something coming up my throat, but I keep talking. "You're not sticking together, Franta. You're not."

"Yeah," a few of the boys say.

Franta squeezes in between Shpulka and Felix and sits back down. Felix starts crying really hard, and Franta hugs him. Felix lets out a loud moan, and I realize I wish I were sitting where he is. Eventually Felix pulls away, crosses his arms on the table, and buries his head there, facedown. Franta places his hand on Felix's back.

"You know," Franta says, "I used to have a cousin. Sasha. Nine years older than me. He lived in Prague. I'm from Brno, so I didn't see him so often, but whenever I did, I always thought, *Wow, Sasha is so old.* One of my first memories is from the weekend of his bar mitzvah. Thirteen might as well have been twenty-five as far as I was concerned. And when we would play soccer together, I felt like I was playing with a member of the national team. And at my bar mitzvah, he made a speech, as the oldest cousin. Just like any other adult. Big cousin Sasha. But do you know something? The last time I saw him, in 1939, I thought, for the very first time, *He's only nine years older than me. Only.* Because I was a man too. The years between us didn't matter so much anymore."

Franta stands up and walks around the table. "Soon you'll be men too. All of you. Soon we'll be peers. A few years from now, you'll be walking down the street, on the way to work, perhaps with a tie around your neck. You will, don't laugh, it happens even to the best of us. And you'll see your old friend, Franta. And we'll stop and have a beer, we will." Franta pats me on the shoulder. I wish he'd keep his hand there forever. "It's what men do sometimes."

"Beer is disgusting," Kikina says.

"They call this one of the boys' rooms," Franta says. "But you're not boys. Not anymore. Not after the last few years. The Nazis stole that from you too. They stole the last years of your childhood from you. You're men already, and you know this. You are men, and as men you will carry on without me. I was only one member of the Nesharim, and the Nesharim are much bigger than one person. All you need to do is support one another and remember how we do things here. That is all. You'll carry on without me, do you understand? And that"—Franta's eyes grow wide and he takes an extra-deep breath—"that includes pillow fights. Even if you are men."

Franta walks over to a ladder, climbs up, and sits down on the top bunk. "Look at you. The Nesharim," he says, clearing his throat. No one says anything for a while, until Franta speaks again, his eyes red. "I love all of you. Like brothers. Every last one of you. Promise me you'll remember that. Promise."

The room is silent. A few of us are still crying, but only a few.

"Franta," Felix finally says. "Is your cousin . . . Sasha . . . is he here? At Terezin?"

Franta doesn't respond, just bites on the inside of his cheek or something and blinks his eyes a few times. "Rim, rim, rim, tempo Nesharim," he whispers. In fact, he whispers it so quietly I'm not sure that's what he said until he whispers it again, no louder than the first time. "Rim, rim, rim, tempo Nesharim."

"Rim, rim, rim, tempo Nesharim." A few of the others join in this time.

"Rim, rim, rim, tempo Nesharim." I say it as well, though it's still barely audible.

"Rim, rim, rim, tempo Nesharim." Everyone's saying it now, but it's still just a whisper. Which somehow, I don't know how, makes it feel more powerful than ever before. Even more powerful than the day we screamed it with everything we had after winning the soccer championship. I close my eyes and hear each person saying it separately and together, our voices mixing and not mixing in the air all at the same time.

"Rim, rim, rim, tempo Nesharim,"

Kikina, Pudlina, Pavel, Brena, Kapr.

"Rim, rim, rim, tempo Nesharim!"

Shpulka, Felix, Pedro, Erich, Extraburt, Kali.

"Rim, rim, rim, tempo Nesharim!"

Grizzly, Pajik, Gustav, Krsya, Franta, and me. Every one of us crying out.

"Rim, rim, rim, tempo Nesh—"

A loud crack interrupts us. The door slamming against the wall. I open my eyes. It's Erich, his cheeks splotchy and red, his eyes half shut in anger.

"It's not fair!" he screams. "It's just not fair!"

At some point Franta has to leave to speak with someone. The room is much too sad without him, so I walk over to the Dresden Barracks to see Mother and Marietta. Terezin seems both deserted and buzzing. There are people walking quickly in every direction, but no one is talking, no one is even looking at anyone else.

"Hey, uh," I ask some woman who I've met a couple of times but can never remember her name, "have you seen my mother?"

"Upstairs," she says and points. "I saw her follow your sister there. To the attic."

"The attic?" I say. "Why would anyone go to the attic?"

But all she tells me is how to get there.

I'm barely at the last stair when I hear someone talking very, very loudly.

"You will not! Put that back now!"

Is that Mother?

"Leave me alone!"

That's definitely Marietta.

I freeze where I am, not because I'm trying to hide, more because of their voices. I've never heard them so furious.

"I will not allow it!" Mother shouts. "Do you hear me? Absolutely not!"

"Try and stop me!"

And then no one says anything. Instead, people breathing hard and groaning and then a few loud thuds. I take a couple of steps forward and turn into the main part of the attic. Mother and Marietta are both on the floor. Mother has her hands on a suitcase that Marietta is reaching for. All around them, and taking up most of the attic, are piles and piles of suitcases. There must be a few hundred at least, in neat stacks nearly reaching the ceiling.

"Give that to me!" Marietta shouts. "It's mine! Give it!"

"What's going on?" I ask. They both look at me like I've caught them doing something they shouldn't be doing. I almost feel like I'm the mother or something. "Why are you fighting?"

Mother fixes her hair, stands up, and straightens her dress. Marietta lunges for the suitcase, but Mother has moved it out of her reach. "It's nothing, Misha," Mother says. "Go downstairs, I'll be there soon. You can tell me about your day."

"Why does Marietta want the suitcase? Where's she going? I thought the transport was for men."

"She's not going anywhere," Mother says, her voice sort of calm and sort of something else.

Just then Marietta leaps up and grabs the suitcase. "I'm going with Gustav," she says, and heads in my direction.

"Stop her," Mother says firmly. "Misha, please, stop her."

"Wait, Marietta, wait," I say, putting my hands up

in the air. "What are you doing? What are you talking about?"

Marietta passes me, but then stops. Without turning around she says, "Gustav's on the transport, and I'm volunteering to go with him."

"Marietta," Mother says, and begins weeping. "Marietta . . . please . . . I'm begging you."

Marietta doesn't say anything. I try to think of something to say, but I can't, and I'm scared anything I do say will make her start walking again. Meanwhile, Mother keeps crying, even as she tries to stand straight and make her face look like the face of someone who isn't crying.

"I love him," Marietta says, with her back still to us. "I want to be with him. I'm volunteering. And that's that."

"Well . . . but . . . but what about us?" I ask.

I see her shoulders rising up and down with each large breath. "I want to be with Gustav." And she starts down the stairs.

Mother rushes past me and grabs Marietta by the arm. "Who have you heard from?" she says to Marietta.

"Leave me alone," Marietta says, ripping Mother's hand from her shoulder and continuing down the stairs.

"Who have you heard from?" Mother repeats the question, this time slower, each word almost its own sentence. "Alena? Nina? Berta? Who? Dita, Marcela, Eva,

Helena, Monika? Have you heard from any of them? Even from one of them? Five months, Marietta, they all left five months ago. We received one postcard from Louise. One. With the script slanting down, Marietta."

"So what?" Marietta turns and looks at us with disgust. "What? Do you think, what, that they're just shooting everyone at the other end of the transport? They could do that to us here and save the trains for something else. Think about it." She turns around. "I'm going with him. It's final." And she starts down the stairs again.

"The last time one of us agreed to go with them," Mother says quickly, her voice making my heart race and Marietta's legs stop, "the last time just one of us went off with them . . ." Mother's hand goes up to her mouth, and I can hear her crying again. "Marietta," she says in almost a whisper, "if you go, and if I don't see you again . . ."

"Don't . . . ," Marietta says. "It's not the same . . . you're not—"

"Marietta," Mother says and walks down a few stairs until she reaches her. She hugs her from behind. "If you love him, and if he loves you," she says softly, "then you'll stay here, where he knows you'll be safe. You're safe here. It's bad here, yes, but you're safe. And if things are okay there, like he says, then when this is all over, you'll find each other. And you'll still love each other. Right?

Wouldn't you want him to do the same if you were the one going? Wouldn't you want him here, where you know he'll be okay?"

Marietta doesn't answer, but Mother doesn't let go of her either. So we all just stand there, until, maybe a whole minute later, Marietta drops the suitcase, which tumbles down a couple more steps and comes to a rest against the wall. Then she walks all the way down the stairs and slams the door behind her.

Mother sits down right where she was standing, so I take the suitcase back up to the attic and place it on top of a short stack of almost identical suitcases. And then I stay up there for a little while longer, until I can hear that Mother is done making these weird noises I've never heard her make before. Noises I hope I don't hear from her again for a long, long, long time.

October 6, 1944

MOTHER TOLD ME NOT TO, SHE TOLD ME
it would just make things worse, but for some reason I can't
help it. I go up to the bashta and wait until it pulls away.
Today's the fourth time I'm doing this. Two days ago I was
probably up here for a couple of hours. But today it looks
like they're more organized, because here it comes. Seventeen cars long. The whole thing rattling and squeaking on
the rails as it rolls out of the camp. To wherever exactly all
these trains keep going. To the East. To the place where
people write postcards with the letters slanting down.

The fifth transport in ten days. Almost ten thousand
people altogether.

And I watch from up here. Because the one time I saw
it from up close, the day Franta left, I knew I would never
do that again.

After I hugged him for the fifth time, after I watched

him hug another dozen Nesharim for the fifth time, he headed for the train. He looked different that day. He looked—I don't know—he looked quiet.

The doors of the wooden cars slid open, but there was nothing inside. Nowhere to sit. Meaning the cars were just long, empty boxes on wheels. And then the guards, kicking and screaming, jammed as many people as possible into each one. More people than seemed possible actually. Like the time nine of us stuffed ourselves into the elevator back in Holesovice. The day it got stuck and Father made us take the stairs for a week.

Now today's train takes a turn, curving past some colorful trees and a long gray building with ten windows, all facing the tracks.

We shouted good-bye to Franta one more time and watched him until he disappeared into a crowd of men disappearing into the fourth box. Where there would be nowhere to sit. And probably nowhere to go to the bathroom, either. They'd all just have to stand there like that, all crammed together until they got to wherever they were going. Which was probably going to take a while, because Poland—which is where everyone says these trains are going—I don't think it's all that close to here.

Tuti and Brena and Gustl are gone now. I even saw Inka, her beautiful red hair tied into a tight ponytail, on her way to a transport a couple of days ago. I went up to her and said, "Bye, Inka," mostly because I never had the guts before. She waved, even though we were only about ten feet away from each other and said, "See you later, Misha." Which almost made me happy, because I always wondered if she actually knew my name.

Gustav's gone too. I haven't seen Marietta since. She goes to work and spends the rest of the day in bed, refusing to speak to anyone.

Oh well, today's train is gone now too.

Bye-bye.

Okay, time to go.

So I head back down and walk through the camp, all the way to the Dresden Barracks, where I'm staying for now. Terezin's so quiet, and so empty. When I got here, almost two years ago, every street and sidewalk was like standing below the astronomical clock in the Old Town Square when it's about to strike noon on a Sunday. People everywhere.

But not anymore.

No one plays under the wooden pavilion anymore. No one sits on any of the benches anymore. Somehow all of this would be a little easier to take if the leaves weren't starting to fall off the trees and the air wasn't getting colder. But winter coming makes it all that much worse.

The Danish men in the bakery—who for some reason weren't sent away when Franta was—they keep telling me and Tommy that this will all end soon. At least I think this is what they're saying. Every day I hear some new rumor about the Allies' progress and how badly the Germans are losing. But it's all secondhand gossip at best, so who knows. And anyway, how badly could the Germans be losing if they're still managing to organize all these trains out of here? If things were really that bad for them, they'd forget about us altogether and concentrate on fighting the other armies. At least that's what I would do, because it's not like we're all that much of a threat or anything.

I enter the barracks and head into my new room. Mother's hanging a wet skirt over a clothesline running between two bunks. By the time it dries, the thing will smell like it needs to be washed again. She looks at me like she wants to ask me where I was, like she wants to yell at me for not listening to her, but she knows there's no point. Because what's she going to do? Send me to my room? I don't have one. Give me extra chores? I work like a dog for hours every day. Threaten me with some other punishment? Yeah, right. What could be worse than this?

So I just go to my bed and lie down. I could read a book or something, but I know I won't be able to concentrate. Because there's only one thought going through my head over and over and over again: If these transports keep up like this, pretty soon I won't be watching from the bashta. In fact, I won't be watching anything at all, because from what I could tell, those cars didn't even have any windows.

Actually, that's not the only thought going through my head. Because there's this, too: If you're willing to put too many people in a train car with nowhere to sit, in a train car without windows, well, then what does that mean? Would you do that if you're really taking people to someplace better? And what if Aunt Louise knew for certain what slanting down meant, and it is worse there?

But worse how? And worse why? I mean, how is it even possible for everything to keep getting worse and worse for over five years now? When are things going to finally start getting better?

And what if they don't?

October 12, 1944

"WHERE DID MOTHER GO?" I ASK MARIETTA, who ignores me as she opens her small bag and rearranges something inside it. After that she looks around the giant, noisy assembly room, like she's waiting for someone else. "C'mon," I try again, "where is she?"

"How should I know?" she snaps back.

"Fine," I say quietly, and lower my eyes, even though I hardly want to see that stupid piece of paper tied around my neck with a string, the number 1385 the only thing printed on it. Marietta's says 1386.

That's out of fifteen hundred. And we're a part of it, because we've finally run out of luck. I guess Father's reputation only saved us for so long.

"Well . . . she better, I don't know, she better hurry," I say. "Because . . . because what if they start loading us and she's not here? Then what happens?"

"What? Are you worried she'll miss the train? If it was that easy not to go, don't you think that's what everyone would do?" Marietta says. "She's on the list, Misha, just like us. We're all going. All of us."

She's right. We are. Our day finally came, like I knew it would. And so now we're in the Hamburg Barracks, in the Schleuse, where everyone reports and then waits and waits and waits. I saw Pavel with his mother before, but now I can't find him. We've been here for a while, because when we arrived, the windows at the other end of the room were these kind of bright squares. But now the squares are pale gray.

Marietta's fussing with her bag again. I have no idea why. I thought she might be happy about winding up on a transport. Because of Gustav. But for some reason she's not, not at all. "Hey," I tell her, "do you want me to take something for you, because I have—"

"Can't you just leave me alone, Misha?" she says, her cheeks growing red. "Just for once?"

"Sorry," I say. "I was just . . . I was . . ." And then I'm trying to concentrate on the big black button on my bag. Just on that. Shiny metal. Four holes.

I'm trying to block out Marietta's voice echoing in my head. I'm trying not to think about the crowd everywhere and how they're going to start loading us into those cars soon. I'm trying not to think about Mother and why she's not here and how it almost doesn't matter where she is and whether she comes back, because one way or another we're all going to be on the next train, which will leave soon. And there's nothing anyone can do about it. Not this time.

Suddenly the only thing I can think about is Father, because for a second I was idiotic enough to think that he would figure something out. Some dumb part of me decided to forget he's gone, hoping he'd know what to do. I actually pictured him in a suit and tie just walking in here and clearing the whole thing up. With his smile and calm confidence.

But it's been almost three years since he cleared anything up.

Just concentrate on the button. Shiny metal. Four holes. Black thread.

And then Marietta's hand is on mine. Her cold, soft hand. "Sorry, Misha," she whispers into my hair, her breath warm. "I'm sorry. She'll be back soon. I know she will."

Shiny metal. Four holes. Black thread. A crooked scratch along the edge.

An hour later, with the gray windows growing dimmer, I see her. Walking swiftly between the clumps of people and heading straight for us. The number 1384 still tied around her neck. But her eyes don't look quite like her eyes anymore. They're open so wide, it looks like they might fall right out of her head. But I can't tell if she's happy or sad or what.

"Come, let's go," she says when she reaches us.

"Go where?" Marietta asks.

But she just says, "Come, let's go, hurry," picks up her bag, and starts walking. So we stand up with our bags and follow her, even though she stops every few steps and touches the end of her left sleeve with her right hand. We wind around the other fatherless families gathered around their bags, until I realize where we're going. Toward those guards at the wooden table in the far corner. Where we first checked in a bunch of hours ago.

At the table two guards are smoking cigarettes and talking casually to each other, as if they weren't in a room with fifteen hundred prisoners waiting for a transport to who knows where. Three German shepherds are sleeping in a spot on the floor behind them. "Excuse me," Mother says to the guards, quietly but firmly. "Excuse me," she says again a few seconds later.

One of them looks up, his face extremely thin, with a long thin scar over his right eye. He says nothing.

Mother inserts two fingers into the long sleeve of her

dress and pulls out what looks like a tube. Then I see that it's actually a rolled-up piece of paper. Looks like a scroll or something. She unrolls it flat on the table and turns it around, pushing it toward the guard. It's just a quarter sheet of paper, with something typed on it. I think I see a signature on it as well. When he goes to grab it, she pulls it back, for just a moment.

"We've been removed," she says. "From the transport—"

"I can read," he says.

"What?" Marietta asks excitedly. Mother shushes her.

The guard elbows the other man, who drops his cigarette, crushes it under one of his shiny boots, and peers over the first guard's shoulder at the paper.

"Go up those stairs"—the second guard points to a door at the far end of the assembly area—"and wait in one of the rooms there. We'll let you know when you can go."

"But," Mother says, taking the paper back, "I'm sorry . . . but . . . it says we're excused from the transport." The first guard tilts his head a bit and flares his nostrils. One of the dogs growls, but doesn't move. Another one opens its eyes. "I'm sorry . . . it's just . . ."

"Upstairs," the first guard says. "Now."

Halfway up the stairs I hear a loud screeching. I run to the top and look out a narrow, barred window. Even though not much light is coming through this window, I can easily make out the train. The three of us squeeze together and watch it slowly rumble past. I try counting the cars but lose track at fourteen.

Mother opens the first door, which is right next to the stairway. A room, around half the size of our old room back in L417. Filled with maybe thirty people, including Pavel and his mother.

"Pavel!" I say.

"Hey, Misha." He waves. And I'm about to go over to him when Mother tugs my arm.

"There's nowhere to sit here. Come," she says.

Marietta walks a bit down the narrow hallway and opens the second door. Pretty much like the first room. Same size, same number of people. I think I see someone I recognize when Mother says, "Misha, go check the third door."

I take a dozen steps, my footsteps echoing off the hard wooden floor and bare walls, until I reach the door, where I stand still for a moment. Somehow it's totally silent here. I turn the knob and look inside. Two young women and a boy maybe half my age. That's it.

"Pretty much empty," I say back to Mother and Marietta. They head over and we go inside, sitting on the floor near one of the far corners. I can't tell if this is the right place to be or not, and I almost ask Mother, until I get a good look at her face. Her eyes are still opened wide like before, but the rest of her face, it almost looks like glass, like if the slightest thing goes wrong, the whole thing might shatter.

"So I asked Mr. Spier," Mother says after we get settled, still clutching the piece of paper, "to please—"

"Mr. Spier?" I ask.

"The head of my department," she says. I try to take the paper from her, but she pulls it away quickly.

"What did he do?" Marietta asks as the door opens. Mother swings her head toward the door, like someone just shot a gun off over there. But all that happens is two women around Mother's age and a girl come inside.

"Mr. Spier," Marietta says. "What did he do?"

"Well," Mother says, squeezing her eyes shut and taking a deep breath, "he went away for a while. And . . . and I simply sat there. Worrying about the two of you." She almost laughs. "I worried that the train would come while I was gone . . . and that when I returned . . ."

"See?" I say to Marietta, who just shakes her head.

"Until he came back. With an SS officer. I had seen him before, a young man with baby blond hair. Very young. He would come to the workshop from time to time to speak with Mr. Spier. Never with anyone else. But today he came straight over to me, Mr. Spier right behind him. 'Herr Richter,' Mr. Spier said. 'Do you recall your enthusiasm for the teddy bears we've been making?' Richter didn't say anything. He just crossed his arms. 'You doubled your order two weeks ago. For Christmas, you said. Do you recall that? For these teddy bears.' And from a table nearby Mr. Spier grabbed one of the bears I had made."

"What do they look like?" I ask.

"Misha," Marietta whines, "what does that matter?"

"It's a small, light brown bear," Mother says. "Furry, of course. Nice round tummy. Black plastic eyes, black nose, little black mouth, almost smiling. Or at least I like to think so. And I sew, for each one, a little flannel shirt with a button near the neck."

Our heads are jerked over to the sound of the door opening. But it's only a woman and a small boy, maybe four years old.

"Mr. Spier handed the bear to Richter," Mother says. "The one I finished yesterday morning, just before they announced the transport. It may have been my best yet."

"What do you mean?" I ask.

Mother shakes her head and looks down at her lap. "Hard to say. But sometimes . . . sometimes the bears—it never happens with anything else I make—but sometimes . . . with the bears, I can almost feel them coming to life. Or no, not exactly that, but I can tell how a little girl or a boy will love them, someday. Marietta, do you remember the doll you had, when you were little?"

"Alexandra," Marietta says softly, and actually smiles.

"How much you loved her," Mother says.

"I'd sit and brush her hair for hours."

"That is what I think about sometimes when I'm making a bear. When I used to make them. That someday a child will talk to it, will share its pillow with the bear each night. Will love it."

"A child with a Nazi for a father," Marietta says. Mother nods her head slightly and rubs her eyes.

There's a noise from below. Maybe dogs barking. Maybe yelling. It comes through the floor and straight into my body, making me stand up, almost like an electric jolt. I walk over to the wall with two small windows, but when I get up on my tiptoes and look out, there's nothing to see. The windows must be facing the wrong direction, because there's nothing more than an empty street below. It's still light out, but I can tell it won't be for long.

"Misha," Mother calls out to me. I go back and sit down.

"So what did Richter do with the bear?" Marietta asks.

"Held it. Squeezed it. Turned it upside down. Inspected it the way only an SS officer would. Like he was looking at a radio or a rifle." Mother uncrosses and recrosses her legs. "Then he nodded his head and looked me up and down, so I lowered my head, of course. But I heard Mr. Spier say, 'This woman, she made that teddy bear. She makes all of them. And she's been placed on the next transport.'"

"I thought you make fake flowers, too," I say.

"They call them 'artificial flowers,' Misha," Mother says. "And I do make them. Or rather, I used to. Because lately, only teddy bears, all day long."

"So what then?" Marietta asks.

"Yes, well, Richter finally spoke. 'Only her?' he asked Mr. Spier. So Mr. Spier told him, 'Occasionally someone else will help her, but it's mostly just her. And she is the best. By far.'"

"Really?" I ask. "Are you?"

"I'm not bad," Mother says, and even smiles for a split second. "But Richter, he merely stood there, still holding the teddy bear."

"A Nazi with a teddy bear," Marietta says, shaking her head.

"So then Mr. Spier said, 'If she goes on the transport, we will not be able to complete your order, at least not with the kind of bears you were planning on giving to your daughters.'"

"Then what?" Marietta asks. But Mother doesn't say anything, because suddenly there are noises from below again. Only louder this time. Screaming and shouting and dogs barking. Plus something else that's hard to figure out. Whatever it all is, it's making the floor vibrate. Probably the sound of fifteen hundred sad and frightened people standing up and heading toward the train. Mother grabs my hand and I let her, squeezing back hard myself. I close my eyes and wait for the floor to stop moving.

"Then what?" Marietta asks again a few minutes later.

"Yes. Well, Richter stood there for a moment or two in silence." Mother swallows and her chest expands. "I tried to do nothing, because I was certain anything I would do or say would be liable to anger him. I sat with my head lowered, sneaking glances up at him, hoping he wouldn't notice. Eventually he said, to Mr. Spier, not to me, he said, 'Okay.'"

"Okay?" I say. "Okay what?"

"Exactly," Mother says just as the sound of dogs barking comes loudly through the floor, like they're directly below us. One of the other kids in our room, a boy I think, starts crying.

"So what happened?" Marietta whispers for some reason.

"Then Mr. Spier said to him, 'But she has two children. If they go, she'll go with them.' Richter handed the bear back to Mr. Spier and crossed his arms, and then I saw him looking at me, so I quickly looked down again. Then, finally, he said, 'Okay, those two as well, but no one else.' And before I could say a word, Mr. Spier led him away into his tiny office."

Mother looks down at her right knee for a while, like she forgot she was in the middle of telling us a story.

"So," I finally say, "so what happened after they came out of his office?"

Mother doesn't answer right away. "Richter," she says slowly, "he left the workshop. Immediately. He never even looked at me again. Instead, Mr. Spier came over and handed this to me." Mother raises the paper a bit. She finally lets me take it from her. One end of the tiny scroll is wrinkled and dented from how tightly she's been holding it.

Though there's barely any light in here at this point, I hold the incredibly thin paper up close to my eyes until I can make out the letters. All it says is:

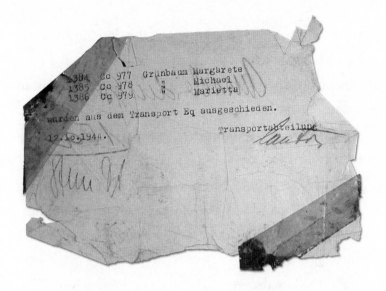

1384 Cc 977 *Gruenbaum Margarete*
1385 Cc 978   "   *Michael*
1386 Cc 979   "   *Marietta*
are excused from the Transport Eq
12.10.1944   Transport Department

And some signature, Richter's probably.

"So then why are we up here?" Marietta asks. "Why didn't they just let us go? It says we're excused. Mother, it says we're excused. What are we doing here?"

But Mother just shakes her head.

I can't sit still anymore, so I get up and walk around the room, even though there's nothing to see or do anywhere.

After a minute or so I walk over to the door and put my ear against it. Nothing. At least at first. But then I hear some clicking, maybe from the stairs, yes it must be from the stairs, because I can hear it getting louder and closer. Then a door opens somewhere down the hall, and a deep voice shouts something.

"What's he saying?" Mother asks.

"I'm not sure," I say. He shouts something again, followed by dogs barking, and now the boy in our room starts crying.

"Shh!" Marietta says to the woman holding him. "You have to shut him up." The woman puts her hand over the boy's mouth and rocks him like he's a much younger kid. For a second he's quiet, and I push my ear against the door trying to figure out what's being screamed.

"Fifty!" the voice says, much louder and much clearer this time. "Fifty more!"

Mother's hand goes up to her mouth. Suddenly all kinds of horrible noises from down the hall begin pouring into our room. Voices, screaming, and dogs barking viciously. I hurry back to Mother and grab her arm, waiting for the dogs to stop. The boy starts in with his crying again. Mother puts her arm around me and grabs Marietta's hand with her other hand. She squeezes me much too tightly.

"All of you!" the voice screams, with the dogs barking a split second after he finishes screaming.

"No!" a woman shouts, completely terrified. "No, no, no! Please!" Again and again she shouts this, though after a while it's more a cry than a bunch of words.

I break free of Mother's grip and run back to the door. "Misha!" she shouts at me in a kind of whisper. But I can't help it. I grab hold of the doorknob and press my ear against the door.

"You!" the same voice orders. "Now!"

Then more vicious barking and crying and begging. And walking. People from that first room must be walking down the stairs. Someone keeps screaming and begging "No, no, no," over and over and over, the dogs answering with their terrifying barks. And then a name, I think, maybe "Gerta," echoing loudly.

Five seconds later the door slams, and then it's completely quiet again, like none of that just happened.

My left hand hurts, and it takes me a few seconds to convince myself to let go of the doorknob. Even then, I can't get the rest of my body to move, so I just stand there, trying not to think at all.

Then, just as I realize I never heard the clicks going down the stairs, I hear them, growing closer. A bunch of clicks. That man's boots and maybe the nails of those dogs, too. I swear I can feel all that clicking as it runs along the floor and up through this door. It's like they're walking along the edge of my ear. Then another door opens.

"Twenty-one! Get up! Move!"

And now I want to get away from the door, but something won't let me, even though I can feel my body shaking.

"Not him, not him!" a woman shouts, begging.

A dog's bark explodes and someone shrieks, bitten probably. The hall fills with children crying and a woman screaming. Their voices are so powerful and so terrified, I feel like I'm hearing them through my skin, like they're cutting straight into me.

A man yells, "Let go of him now!" And then loud footsteps and a deep, hard thud, like a body hitting the wall between our rooms. For a second the screaming stops, only to start up again even louder. Layers and layers of screaming, all of it making my entire body tremble.

"Over there, all of you!" a man shouts above the screaming and the barks of the dogs cutting through the air.

All of you. Does that mean he's taking everyone from that room? And if it does, then our room is next, because he's definitely just down the hall. He's definitely in the room right by ours. And so if he needs any more, our room is next! He'll click down the hall and swing our door open, the dogs growling and snapping at us. He'll say "thirteen" and that will mean all of us. And we'll beg like those other people begged, but it won't matter, because they don't care about begging, they don't care about anything, because if they're fine stuffing one hundred people into a boxcar with no seats and no windows, why would they care at all about people begging?

Because people who stuff other people into train cars, they don't care about any of the things you're supposed to care about. The only things they care about are their teddy bears and their numbers, and so if they need all of us, they take all of us. They'll take every last one of us. And if that's all they care about, then who knows what the slanting postcard really meant. Maybe it is really, really bad wherever the transport goes. Maybe it's the worst place ever, and so maybe there's a reason why that's the last postcard Aunt Louise sent. And maybe we're about to find out why.

The shrieking and barking and fighting continue pouring in from the next room, but somehow I pull myself away from the door and rush over to Mother. I bury my head into her stomach. She holds me tight, but it doesn't really help, because I can feel how every muscle in her body is tensed, waiting for the clicks and the barks and a number that is much too large for our practically empty room to be screamed from the doorway. I feel Marietta hug me from behind, trying to reach out for Mother, too.

Marietta is crying, making a horrible sound that causes the eight-year-old Marietta to appear in my head.

I don't want Louise to be right. I don't want slanting down to mean what Mother said it means. I don't want the door to open and the dogs to put me on that train. I don't want to sit on bare floors waiting for something horrible to happen. I don't want to be here anymore, to be a helpless prisoner who can only hope for there to be no more numbers. I push my head farther into Mother's stomach, asking it to make all this go away, asking it to make the last five years go away, begging for that train to pull away without us on it, begging for all trains everywhere to disappear forever.

And then, suddenly, silence. Just the screaming and barking and crying still echoing in my head.

I pull my head away from Mother to make sure. And then I hear it, again. The clicking, only this time it's definitely going away from us, that man and those dogs, clicking down the stairs, until it's completely quiet. I've never heard such silence before in my whole entire life.

We sit tightly together, the three of us, in complete darkness. I have no idea how much time is passing. Sometimes it feels like hours, but then I notice Marietta's breath, and I realize that maybe it's only been a few minutes. If I bend my head just right, I can hear something coming through the windows. Nothing specific, just some kind of dull rumble, which gets louder and then quieter again. Sometimes a very loud shout breaks through, but the actual words get lost.

Is the clicking going to return? And if it does, will it reach our door this time? What if the clicking opens our door and screams "Six," then what happens then? Will we have to fight to see who goes and who stays? Because there's nowhere to hide here at all, we're just in the middle of the floor. And what if it's one of the guards from before, the one who told Mother he can read? What if he was insulted and remembers that? Will he get to our room and choose us? Will he come looking for us? Will he grab the paper from Mother and tear it up into pieces, the dogs showing their teeth and snapping at us until he drags us all away?

Or will he take just Mother or Marietta.

Or just me?

My ears stretch out toward the door, like giant antennae, trying to detect those boots clicking up the stairs, while my brain tries to guess what number he'll shout when he opens our door next. I might be praying, even though I don't think I ever understood what praying is. But I'm asking, begging for something.

Please, don't let them come and take us.

Please, anything but that clicking.

Please, just silence.

Please.

But then I hear something. Only it's not clicking or barking or horrified people screaming. Instead, it's the sound of something squeaking and screeching. Metal grinding against metal. It lasts for maybe a minute or two, and then it's gone. And then absolute silence. Nothing but the sound of our exhausted breathing filling the room.

The train, it's gone.

"Come," Mother says some time later.

I may have been sleeping, facedown on the floor. I think I hear her standing up, but I'm not certain. The room is pitch-black. I get up and hear Marietta doing the same. We walk toward the door, and it takes a while, but eventually I find the knob and turn it. There's a very dim glow in the hallway, coming from the stairwell I think, so we walk toward it, followed by the others who were waiting with us. When we get to the next room, we stop, and Mother opens the door.

"Hello?" Mother whispers. "Hello?"

"Yes?" someone says, barely louder than a whisper.

"The train, it departed," Mother says. "It's gone."

Slowly about ten people come out from the room, everyone clutching someone else. Even in the dim light I can barely stand to see the looks on their faces. They look like ghosts, or people who spent the last few hours with ghosts.

We walk down the hallway, not even bothering to check the first room. When we get to the stairwell, we pause briefly and then go down carefully. For a few seconds we pause at the door separating us from the main assembly room. Mother turns the knob and opens the door just a bit, so little I can't even see. Then she opens it wide.

The massive assembly room, lit dimly by a single bulb someone has left on, is completely deserted.

Mother reaches up to her neck, rips off the number, and tears it to pieces. She holds the small scraps in her hand for a moment, and then, I swear, she stuffs them into her mouth and begins chewing. We all do the same. The paper tastes a little bit sweet. And then, spitting out bits of damp paper as we go, we walk back to the Dresden Barracks.

We sigh. We managed to survive another day, thanks to Mother's persistence. And thanks to a stroke of good luck—by the time we arrived on the second floor of the assembly area, there was no space left in the first two rooms next to the stairway.

For some reason, even though it's late, I'm sure no one will bother to stop us, maybe because our path crosses right by Mother's workshop, where she'll go tomorrow morning to continue making more adorable teddy bears for the sons and daughters of the SS.

February 11, 1945

MOST DAYS TOMMY AND I TAKE TURNS telling jokes, it doesn't matter how bad they are. Or describing incredible goals Czechoslovakia will score in the next World Cup. Anything to keep from getting bored. But not today. Not right now. All we're doing right now is trying to find a way to take one step and then another. Thankfully the bakery is only a few blocks away.

The problem is this snow. About a foot of it fell a couple of days ago. Then it warmed up a bit, then it got really cold, and now the streets are half slush and half ice. All this dirty whitish stuff on the ground makes the wagon feel twice as heavy, even now, when it's empty.

So I let myself close my eyes and just push. Every once in a while I open them, to make sure we're going straight. When I look over, I notice Tommy doing the same.

I can only feel the big toe on my left foot. I have no idea if the other nine toes still exist. Yesterday was pretty much the same thing. And the day before that. I really, really hate it here sometimes.

But at least there haven't been any transports for a while. Not since the end of October.

The amazing thing is, it's actually possible to sleep like this. Standing up, walking, pushing, and sleeping. All at the same time.

I think I had a dream. Just now, a really short one. I owned King of Railroads, but we didn't sell trains, just hosted birthday parties.

I haven't had a real birthday celebration this decade, and it's almost half over.

We put the candles in frosted rolls, back at King of Railroads, in my dream. And sang "Happy Birthday" in Danish, even though I don't know Danish.

Kikina, Pajik, Extraburt, Shpulka, and me. We're the only Nesharim still here. But except for Kikina, I don't see any of them most days. Our old room doesn't exist, and it's been too cold to play outside.

Everyone else is gone. Gorila, Pavel, Robin, Majoshek,

Felix, Pudlina, Grizzly, Eli, Jila, Erich, Jindrich, Koko, Leo, Kalisek, Kuzma. And Franta. All gone. Franta last September, and all the rest by the end of October.

And a bunch of others, too, whose names I already forgot.

The one with the bushy eyebrows. What was his name?

Something is bouncing around in the wagon. A roll we missed. Or maybe Tommy schlojsed it. I'm hungry, because I'm always hungry, but I'm too tired to chew.

Mazr? Was that his name? Pretty sure it was something with an M. Definitely had bushy eyebrows. And used to cough a lot.

Something's buzzing way overhead, but I don't care. I only care if I hear a siren. Every few days there's an air raid. Every few days there's a new rumor. The Soviets are in Poland. The Americans are in Germany. Any day now, any day now, any day now.

But right now it feels like I'll be doing this forever. In twenty years I'll still be pushing this wagon. And even though I'll be thirty-four years old, I'll still look like I'm ten, because something about this place keeps me from growing. I'm pretty sure I'm wearing the same pants I wore the day I arrived, which would be falling down past my butt right now if it weren't for this belt.

Or was it Mautner? Martin? He definitely coughed a lot, whoever he was.

"No, don't . . . ," Tommy mumbles. His left shoulder bounces up and down. "Stop, it's . . . just don't . . ."

Or maybe it's twitching. He's definitely talking in his sleep. Like he did two days ago. I think I heard once that you shouldn't wake someone when they're talking in their sleep. But it doesn't matter, because here's the bakery. He'll wake up once we get there, because he always does whenever the wagon comes to a stop.

Mazr. I think it was Mazr. I'll ask Kikina when his wagon gets here. He has a better memory than me anyway.

Kikina, hey, do you remember the kid with the bushy eyebrows and the cough? That's what I'll ask him. *He was pretty good at chess, do you remember?*

Mazr. Mazr?

Well, wherever he went and whatever his name is, I hope his boots are warmer than mine.

April 20, 1945

"DO YOU HEAR THAT?" I ASK TOMMY AND Kikina.

"It's a train, isn't it?" he says.

We're in the bakery, not too far from where the tracks enter Terezin, almost done loading up our wagon for another delivery. Rudi, the boy Kikina usually delivers with, is sick, so the three of us are working together today. I look around to make sure none of our Danish bosses is looking. They must be on a break somewhere, so I run out, Tommy and Kikina following me.

Yup, it's definitely a train, which isn't the most unusual thing, since there's been a slow trickle coming in all this year. But almost all of those trains have been pretty short, usually with fewer than one hundred people on them. Jews who married non-Jews, or those people's children, or something like that. That's who's still being brought here.

On short trains filled with just a few dozen Jews or half Jews who were for some reason protected until the Nazis decided they weren't going to be protected anymore.

But this doesn't look like one of those trains, because this one is at least a dozen cars long.

As we get closer, I realize that all the cars are open. Like the kind you'd use for lumber or coal. But there are people in them anyway. Bald people.

We run alongside the train while it slows down. Because it's moving, I'm having trouble figuring out what it is I'm seeing. Everyone is definitely bald, which is weird enough by itself, but there's something else about them. Something that's making me wish those Danish bakers had caught us when we decided to run off.

Tommy and Kikina are seeing it too. Because neither one is moving anymore. The train is still crawling ahead, but the two of them are standing motionless, their mouths hanging open, their eyes slowly following all those heads. Meanwhile, other people are running up to the train, which finally creaks to a stop. I notice a woman I've seen before, I think she works in the Dresden Barracks kitchen. Yes, it's her, the nicest woman in all of Terezin. Somehow she's always smiling and telling everyone to have a nice day, almost like she doesn't realize where we are.

But right now she's not smiling. She's got her hand up

to her mouth. Then the other one follows and her eyes close. A few seconds later they open, and then, just like that, she faints.

Tommy's holding my sleeve.

"C'mon," he says.

"Okay," I say, but my feet won't move.

And where did Kikina go?

We're maybe only twenty feet from one of the cars, but my body won't let me move any closer. A couple of passengers have gotten off on their own, and I'm trying not to see them. They're two men—at least I think they're men—but they don't really look like people. Both of them are wearing uniforms, white with blue stripes, though they're so filthy I'm not so sure about the white part. And one of them is only wearing pants. I get a good look at his chest, but it doesn't look like a real chest. There just isn't enough of it, at least not for the size of the bald head attached to it. He's walking toward us, and I keep expecting him to snap in half every time he takes a step. He's a skeleton wrapped in skin.

I'm trying to turn away, but he sees me looking at him. Plus he's only about ten feet from us now. His cheekbones push much too far out of his face, and one of his eyes is swollen shut. I can hear him breathing, or maybe that's moaning.

Three feet away from me he stops. His mouth opens, showing me a half dozen rotting teeth. That's it. The rest is just blackness and gums. For a few seconds he stands there, like a person, or a skeleton, getting ready to say something. I feel my mouth opening like his, but I have no idea what to say. Finally I hear a sound come out of his.

"Water." I can't tell if it's a question or a statement. "Water."

Tommy and I race back toward the bakery, no one saying a word. As soon as we get inside, I look around for a cup or mug or a bottle, but I can't find anything.

"How about this?" Tommy asks. He's holding the kind of pot Mother used to make soup in.

"Yeah, okay," I say. We're filling it up at the sink when one of the main bakers, Mr. Haber, walks in.

"What is this?" he asks, already angry.

But we don't stop. Once we're done, we turn off the water and start running out. "There's a train," I say. "Just arrived . . . it's . . . it's . . . it's really . . . go look."

We run back to the train, each of us with a hand on the heavy pot. The water sloshes around, and some of it spills over the rim, so we have to slow down to a quick walk, which unfortunately gives me much too clear a view of the whole train and everything around it. There are people everywhere, people from Terezin and people from the train. People on stretchers and people lying in the grass. And even though we're half the length of a soccer field away, I can tell that the man who asked for water isn't that different from the rest of them. They're skeletons, every last one of them.

"Where did he go?" Tommy asks me.

"How should I know?"

We're standing where I think we were standing before, but the man with the swollen eye is nowhere to be found. I don't think I see the other one either. But then three smaller people, a little bigger than me, notice the pot and hurry to us. One slips and falls silently to the ground. The others don't seem to notice, in fact they don't even seem to notice me and Tommy, just the pot. They grab it from us and it almost tips over, but luckily Tommy and I are strong enough to take it back from them.

"Hold on," I say. "We'll pour it."

And just like that, like they've done this before or something, they kneel down. One of them has no pants at all, he's naked down there, and his thighs sort of look like an old rubber band. He opens his mouth and closes his eyes. While Tommy and I raise the pot and slowly tip it over, I notice a couple of small, oval bugs clinging to the edge of the man's eyelid.

We do this a bunch of times, running from the train

to the bakery and back again, delivering water. It's a stupid system, since a bunch of the water always winds up on the ground, but at least it gives us an excuse to escape every few minutes. I keep telling myself, whenever we get to the bakery, that since I already know what they look like, it doesn't make any sense to be surprised each time we return. But it doesn't help, because I am. Especially by their skin, which is the worst part.

They're all covered with sores, with bugs, with bright red cuts, with infections spitting out pus.

And there's something about their bald heads and their weird eyes, because I can barely tell who's a man and who's a woman, or who's a teenager and who's an adult.

So it's good to run off every few minutes, and I bet Tommy feels the same, even though neither of us has really said much since this all started.

Also the smell is starting to get stuck in my nose. It took me a while to figure out what it reminded me of. Then, all of a sudden, I remembered. The summer our refrigerator broke. These people, they stink like rotting meat.

Around the tenth time we come back with water, I notice that some of the people getting taken off in stretchers are winding up in a pile at the far end of the train. The kind of pile you would never put a living person in.

We empty the pot and are about to go back to the bakery, when I think I hear someone behind me say my name.
So I turn around. Some small person, another skeleton,
looking right at me.

"Misha." Almost like a question.

"Uh-huh," I say, trying not to stare at the red spots all
over this person's scalp.

"Misha." And a bony hand reaches up to the scalp, so I
try looking at the elbow instead, but it's much too pointy.

"Yeah," I say, and force myself to look at this person's
eyes. I still can't figure out if it's a boy or a girl, but I'm
pretty sure it's not an adult. The eyes are moving in weird
ways, like the person doesn't know how to focus anymore.

"Inka," the person says weakly. "I'm Inka." For some
reason I turn to Tommy, like maybe he can help. "I'm Inka."

I look at the grass for a moment and say the name to
myself. *Inka.* A tremor rushes down the side of my body. I
look at her. I think she's trying to smile, but only half her
face seems like it's working.

Just then Kikina walks up to us, a smaller pot in his
hand. "Hey," he says to me. I groan something. "I don't
think we should keep bringing them water. These people,
they need food." But I don't answer him. I'm staring at
Inka, trying to find Inka. "How much bread is in the bakery,
Misha? Wait, what if they can't chew? What do you think?"

I can't find her. "C'mon, Misha, what should we do?"

"It's Inka," I finally tell him, my voice cracking. "Remember?" She presses her lips together, and some blood escapes from a long crack in the top one. "Inka. With the beautiful red hair. Beautiful Inka. Remember?"

Mr. Hertz is waiting for us back in the bakery. "What you doing?" he says to us angrily in the weird Danish-Czech-German he speaks. "Take bag. Go down, in Hamburg Barracks, in *keller*. Down, in basement. Potatoes. Bring many potatoes."

"Potatoes?" Tommy asks.

"Now. Yes. Go!"

It takes us a while, but eventually we find a dank storage room filled with giant bins of potatoes. Some are rotten, but most seem okay. So we each put about forty in the burlap sacks we brought with us and rush back to the bakery.

When we get there, we find another five people already at work. One of them is Mr. Wolff, the head baker. The rest I don't know.

"Knives, go," Wolff says to the three of us. "To peel, now."

We start peeling. Then Wolff gives me a flat metal thing with holes in it. "You, you." And he takes a potato and runs it back and forth over the metal thing. Thin strips of potato come out from the bottom.

"You want me to grate them?" I say.

"Yes, yes. Grate, you," he says. "And then—" He points to a huge pot of water sitting on top of a gas flame. "Into there. Yes?"

For the next hour, we peel, grate, boil, and mash the potatoes. When we run out of potatoes, we grab the sacks, go back to the Hamburg Barracks, and get more. After we finish mashing the potatoes, and adding a little flour, Wolff or Hertz takes a metal tray, scoops out a bunch of the mash, and makes a flat layer of the stuff across the whole tray. Then he sticks it in the oven.

"Baking potatoes?" Kikina asks. "Why not just give them bread?"

"Too hard," Mr. Hertz says, pointing at his mouth. "They no, uh, no *tander*."

"No teeth?"

"Right, no teeth." He shakes his head and mumbles to himself, "No teeth."

The first few batches are done. The three of us place the trays on our wagons and cover those with sacks, and head out.

"Wait," Mr. Hertz says. He hands Kikina a long knife.

"Cut so same size. Same size. Same. Careful. Very careful."

We push the wagon out into the ghetto, realizing we don't know where we're going. Then Tommy says, "Over there."

On the grass that leads up to the bashta, we see a bunch of them, around thirty or so. We roll the wagon over to them. I try not to look at one of them, because his whole body is twitching like it's ten degrees below zero.

"Now what?" Tommy whispers.

"We have potatoes. Potatoes," I announce. A few of them don't seem to hear, but most spring to attention, and about half actually stand up and hurry toward us. They're all talking, many of them in languages I don't understand. Pushing one another, they crowd around the wagon, almost knocking the whole thing to the ground.

"Get back!" Kikina shouts, and actually raises the knife. A few fall back, while one very tall man actually raises his fist, which shakes so badly I reach up to make it stop. "Sit," Kikina says. "Everyone gets." But almost no one sits. Kikina starts cutting. "Misha," he whispers, "tell me if they're not the same size. I don't want them to attack each other, or us, for getting smaller pieces."

So Kikina cuts while Tommy and I hand out the pieces. Most people don't move once they get their piece. They just stand or sit right where they get it, chewing quickly or very, very slowly. A number of them make a weird sound, something between a moan and a groan.

Once everyone has a piece, we push the wagon off toward another group gathered in the grass about two hundred feet away. But then I notice Tommy isn't with us. I turn back and see him with the first group. He's on the ground next to what I think is a woman. She's lying on her side, her bald head half buried in the grass. Tommy's holding her piece, breaking it into smaller portions, and gently placing one of them into her mouth every ten seconds or so.

On our next delivery I see Marietta off in the distance, running from group to group. As she gets closer to us, I can tell she's upset. Her face is red and her arms are moving about frantically. I leave Tommy and Kikina and race over to her.

"Marietta?"

She notices me but turns away.

"Marietta." And I know it's a stupid question right at this moment, but I ask it anyway. "What's wrong?"

"Gustav," she says. "No one . . . no one knows anything about him. Except this one man, and he said . . . he said he probably . . ." But she doesn't say anything more, just covers her face with her hands, and crumbles to the ground crying.

April 22, 1945

"OW!" KIKINA SHOUTS, BUT I CAN BARELY hear him over the rain, which sounds like it's attacking the ground.

"What?" I ask loudly, and then something hits me, too. "Ow! What is that?"

"It's hailing!" Tommy screams. "C'mon, hurry up!"

We push the wagon quickly toward the Dresden courtyard and hide under the entranceway. For a short while these barracks were my home, but not anymore. Because Dresden is one of the quarantine buildings now, packed with the people who arrived two days ago. Plus a ton more who arrived, on foot, earlier today. I heard they walked all the way from Poland. From the other camps there. From Birkenau, and from places I had never heard about before, Auschwitz and Bergen-Belsen. I guess the Soviets finally reached those camps, so the Germans closed them down and sent the prisoners back in our direction.

Most of them were wearing these horrible wooden shoes, and when I saw one of them remove his . . . well, when I saw his feet, I made up some excuse that I had to go back to the bakery. When I got there, I spent a few minutes in this little storage space, where no one could see me.

The hail bounces off the pavement, and the noise echoes ferociously off the cement all around us. We stand there, not talking, because we wouldn't hear one another anyway. A little gust blows past, and I get a nice whiff of the potatoes. We've been making deliveries for around forty-eight hours, but most people still grab their piece like they've never ever seen food before. Every time we return to the bakery, there are more volunteers helping out, peeling potatoes, grating potatoes, delivering potatoes. But we still can't keep up. Not even close.

A few minutes later the rain dies down a little, so we each grab a tray, and hurry inside.

"Thank you," a woman with pale green eyes says to me in Czech as I hand her the last piece in my tray.

"You're welcome," I say.

It looks like she's about to say something else, but she

just takes a bite instead. She chews slowly, and after she swallows, she almost looks like a normal person. A terribly thin, extremely weak person, but a real person. Not a skeleton.

So I ask her the question I've been meaning to ask every one of the people we've been feeding for the last two days.

"Where were you?" I ask.

She takes another bite, chews, and swallows. "Auschwitz," she says.

"But I thought," I say, checking to see where Kikina and Tommy are, "I thought the transports went to Birkenau."

"Same thing," she says.

"But so . . . ," I start to say, not sure what I want to ask. "What was there? What happened?" She keeps chewing slowly, ignoring me. So I ask her another question, one that started bothering me yesterday afternoon. "And why didn't any kids or old people come back with you? What happened to them?"

"Gas," she says, and picks up a bit of potato that landed on her forearm, not far from a spot where six black numbers are written across her skin. "And then"—she swallows—"up the chimney."

"What?" I lean in closer. "What does that mean?"

But all she does is reach her bony hand out to me and run her finger down my cheek. It gives me the chills, but I let her do it a few times anyway.

Many hours later the three of us are pushing the wagon through some puddles when Kikina and I break the silence at almost the same time.

"Did you guys—" he starts saying.

"Hey, what does 'up the chimney' mean?" I ask.

"What?" Tommy asks.

"Some woman," I say, "back in Dresden. She said something about people going up chimneys."

Kikina nods his head. "I heard my mother say the same thing yesterday. But she stopped talking when she saw me."

"And gas," Tommy says. "I keep hearing people talk about gas."

Now we're just standing behind our wagon in the middle of the ghetto. "This woman," I say, "she said gas, then chimney."

For some reason I think of Mother. Everyone has been working so hard, the second we lie down for the night we're out cold. So I haven't talked to her almost at all in two days. Which normally would be fine, because a lot of the time, ever since I started working in the bakery actually, I've liked being on my own. But right now, I wouldn't mind if she just showed up all of a sudden.

"And have you noticed," I say to the guys, "no old people? And no kids, either. Inka, who's a couple of years older than us, she's probably the youngest person we've seen."

"Though it is pretty hard to tell," Tommy says.

"No, but he's right," Kikina says. "I haven't seen any-one younger than us. I'm sure of it."

Tommy starts pushing the wagon, and soon we're pass-ing by a row of trees with new leaves on them. "Does that mean," Kikina says, "that, you know, Felix and Gorila and Leo and everyone . . . well, what does that mean?"

"And Franta," I say, "what about him?"

"He's older," Tommy says. "So . . . maybe, right?"

"And Pudlina and Grizzly and Eli and . . ."

We push the wagon in silence for a while.

"Gas, then chimney," I say, trying to picture some-thing in my head. But I don't see anything, just feel a dark, heavy lump in the middle of my chest.

"No, no, no. No way," Kikina says. "No way, not even the Nazis would."

"What do you mean, no way?" I say, almost shouting. "Have you looked at those people? The one's who've been eating our potatoes like they've never eaten in their entire lives? Have you? C'mon, anyone who would do that to all those people, who would let them wind up like this, who would just stick them on cars meant for coal, or make them walk as far as they just walked . . . what wouldn't they do? Think about it."

No one talks the rest of the way to the bakery.

"Wonderful news," Mr. Hertz says when we get back, a giant grin on his face. We look at him like he just arrived from another planet. "Red Cross, not Nazis, in charge."

"What?" we all ask.

"Nazis . . . they . . ."—he makes a motion with both his hands—"soon they give it. Terezin. To new man in charge. Dunant. Red Cross. Swiss man."

"I don't believe you," Kikina says. "It's not true."

"True, true," Mr. Hertz says. "Not Rahm. Not Germans."

"What do you mean," Tommy asks. "Are the Germans just gone? Can we leave? Is it over?"

"No, no, not over," Mr. Hertz says. "Not so much yet. Soon, soon."

"You're lying," Kikina says.

Mr. Hertz turns around and walks toward the ovens. He pulls out a couple of trays of potatoes and places them on our wagon. "Don't believe." He shrugs his shoulders. "Okay, don't. Bring potatoes instead. People still very hungry. Go, go, go."

May 2, 1945

"BUT I DON'T WANT TO PLAY CARDS," I say to Mother. "Why can't I go outside?"

"Because," she says, folding a skirt and putting it on a shelf, "I told you a half dozen times already. Nora said that the German soldiers, the ones retreating past Terezin, she said they've been firing into the camp. Just for sport. So if you don't have to be outside, you stay in here. And no, Misha, that is not up for negotiation. You stay here."

"Here" is the Hamburg Barracks, where they stuck us once they cleared out the Dresden Barracks. I swear, half of Terezin is quarantined at this point. More and more people keep arriving from the East, almost every day. Terezin seemed pretty much deserted a few weeks ago, but not anymore. And a bunch of the new arrivals have typhus, which someone said explains the red spots. And the high fever and a bunch of other symptoms too. The

Nazis are terrified of it. I don't know anyone who's seen an SS officer or even a regular German soldier in a long time. Some people think most of them are gone already.

"But this deck is missing two eights, a five, a ten, and the Queen of Diamonds. What's the point?" Mother ignores me. "And what about Marietta? She's not here. Why does she get to leave?"

"She's staying in Block F, with some friends. And she promised me that she would not go out either." Of course Mother lets Marietta do what she wants. I guess a few days after people from the East started returning she finally found someone who recognized Gustav's name. But then this person just started shaking his head. That's all Mother will tell me about what happened, and I'm not sure I'm ready to ask Marietta myself.

Mother picks up a ratty dress from the foot of her bed. "So, tell me, how is Kikina doing?"

"How should I know?" I double-check the cards again, hoping I'm somehow wrong about everything that's missing. "I'm pretty sure he's in the infirmary, but I don't even know what he has. So long as it's not typhus."

Mother removes a small piece of paper from a pocket of her dress. "Well, I think it's quite extraordinary what you boys did. Delivering potatoes from dawn to dusk for over a week." She reaches under the bed and pulls out a small cardboard box, opens it, and puts the piece of paper inside.

"What's that?" I ask.

"Just some things."

"Things? What things?" I get up and go over. The box is half-filled with pieces of paper. "What is all that stuff?"

"Think how many lives you saved, Misha," she says. "You boys are heroes, you are. I'm just glad you didn't catch whatever poor Kikina got. Thank God the Red Cross is here now."

I pick up a few pieces of paper. "Careful," Mother says. A meal ration card, a work assignment, and a small drawing of someone in a kitchen. "Okay, okay," Mother says, and takes them from me, returns them to the box, and puts the whole thing back under the bed.

"What are you saving all that stupid stuff for?" But Mother doesn't answer, just smiles and does something to my hair. I'm about to tell her to stop when all that paper reminds me of something. "Hey, you know, today, when Tommy and I were passing by Q414, there was smoke and paper in the air, and—"

"You shouldn't be going near that building, you know that."

"What's the big deal?" I say. "I heard the SS are gone already. I mean, didn't you just say the Red Cross is here?"

"Yes, but, well, I'm not sure who's really in charge, or even who's still here," Mother says. "Some people say

Rahm is here somewhere, along with some of his men."

"Well, anyway," I say, "a couple of pieces of paper landed near us. So we picked them up. One of them, it said something like 'Herman Lowe,' and then a date, 1901. I don't remember the exact day. Maybe January third or something like that. And then, part of it was cut off, from the fire, but I could still see another date. October seventeenth, 1943, I think." Mother walks over to where I was sitting before and picks up the cards. "We found a few pieces with dates like that. Why are they burning all that paper?"

Mother starts shuffling and motions for me to come over. "This is going to end soon," she says, "and when it does"—she deals me some cards—"people will be held accountable, because—"

But then I hear a bunch of planes buzzing overhead. I rush over to the window and look out. Tommy once told me what the Allies' planes look like, but I can never tell the difference.

"Come, Misha," Mother calls. "Let's play already."

I keep looking out the window. At least twenty silver planes flying overhead in formation. I decide they belong to the Americans. "But I'm sick of all the games we know. I'm sick of being stuck in here. When is this going to end already?"

"Fine," she says, "so we'll make something up. A brand-new game that needs only forty-seven cards."

May 8, 1945

"NO," I TELL TOMMY, "NOT UP TO THE bashta. My mom is going to be mad enough."

"Fine," Tommy says, kicking the ball against the side of a building. It could really use some air, but a ball's a ball. I found it in the basement of our building, where I went snooping around right after dinner, because I couldn't think of anything else to do. The second I found it I raced over to where Tommy's staying.

"How about this?" I say. "We'll practice shooting. Below that line and between those windows. That's a goal."

So we do that for a while, taking turns, and trying it with and without goalies. It's not as fun as a real game, but it's okay. Plus some other boys, a little older than us, show up. They don't speak Czech, but it doesn't matter, because pretty soon we're playing two-on-two in the middle of the street.

Suddenly we hear a bunch of noise. People shouting.

From the direction of the train tracks. And I can't make out a single thing anyone is saying, but somehow the voices sound different from the normal shouting you hear around here.

"C'mon," I say to Tommy, and we start running. The sounds get louder and louder, and more and more people are joining us in the street, including people who I think came from the East, in baggy clothes and barefoot, their hair just beginning to grow back in.

I notice Marietta up ahead, and I yell her name extra loud. I haven't seen her in a few days. She turns around but doesn't stop running, so I put my head down and really sprint until I get to her. "Hey," I say, and grab her hand. I'm barely able to speak I'm breathing so hard. "What . . . why is everyone running?"

Right then we turn a corner, and I see it. Big and green, with a red, five-pointed star up by the main cannon.

A Soviet tank, rolling through Terezin.

"Oh my—"

Marietta pulls me toward her and presses me into her chest, her arms wrapped tight around me. "We're free, Misha," she breathes loudly into my ear. "We're finally free."

A few Russian soldiers appear from out of the tank, and the crowd cheers loudly. Some people begin singing the Czech national anthem, soon joined by dozens and dozens of others, including us. The soldiers smile, and the moment our song ends, they begin singing what must be their own. Two more tanks arrive, and the next thing I know the soldiers are passing out candy and cigarettes. Meanwhile, the crowd grows thicker and thicker, the singing and cheering louder and louder.

It's over. It's finally over.

After a few minutes, and a few pieces of candy, I start walking away from the commotion. Part of me isn't thinking about where I'm going, but part of me knows. I get to the tracks and walk past them until I see the gate, which is wide open and completely unattended.

I reach it and continue walking.

Until I'm not in Terezin anymore.

I find a small rock and sit down, looking out at nothing in particular. Trees, a few houses, the mountains off in the distance. Another couple of tanks roll past, the tops of Russian soldiers waving out to me from their open hatches.

And then it gets very quiet.

It takes me a while to realize I'm still breathing quickly for some reason. So I sit there longer, trying not to think about the fact that Mother will be wondering where I've disappeared to, until my lungs finally relax.

And that's when it hits me. Despite the candy, despite

all the bread I've schlojsed over the last half year, despite all the treats I've traded for with all the bread I've schlojsed. An incredible hunger, unlike anything I've ever felt before. My entire body is hungry. My guts, my toes, my fingers—I swear I can feel it in my hair. For food, for real food, for everything and anything at all.

I almost jump up, because I have a weird urge to go run and find Mother, to tell her, or even not tell her. Just to be with her. But I stay where I am, watching some birds, almost enjoying this strange, intense hunger that only keeps growing.

And then, even though the hunger doesn't go away, something else grabs my attention. Father. I'm trying to remember his face, to remember exactly how it looked, the way his teeth would shine when he smiled, the way the edges of his eyebrows would rise up at the very same time. But I can't see it all, so I convince myself that somewhere, maybe in another box Mother has hidden somewhere else, some pictures of him are waiting for us.

I sit for a while longer. And as dusk arrives, I let myself think about how badly I wish I could tell Father what this all feels like right now, even though I don't have the words for almost any of it. But so what, because I'm sure Father would understand what this incredible hunger is all about, I'm absolutely sure he would.

Epilogue
Prague, Czechoslovakia

December 17, 1945

"MISHA," MOTHER YELLS TO ME FROM the kitchen, "there's a letter for you." I toss down the sports section of the newspaper and hurry down the hallway. In our old building. Back in Holesovice. Not the exact same apartment, but the same building is still pretty good.

Mother's standing by the counter in a bright new dress. And I'm pretty sure she put on that dark red lipstick within the last two minutes. She holds the letter out to me, and as I take it, I notice something sad in her face. Maybe this is just what the mail does to her these days. Because we get way more bad news than good. Mostly about people, about all the people who didn't make it back like us. Including Gustav and Jiri and just about all the other Nesharim. The East was much, much worse than we ever could have imagined.

And if that weren't bad enough, a few weeks ago a

letter arrived telling us that all the valuables Mother had sent to London at the start of the war were in a warehouse that was completely destroyed by a German bombing.

After she cried for a while, she wiped her face and told us we should be happy for what we have. She's been saying that a lot lately, but sometimes her face tells me that she doesn't quite believe it herself, at least not yet. It doesn't help that some of the people here in Prague who kept things for us didn't seem all that happy to see us return. A few of them even denied we gave them anything in the first place. Marietta told me that there's some kind of dumb joke going around in Prague, something that ends with people saying, "My bad luck: Unfortunately my Jew came back too."

I grab the letter and glance at the return address. Brno. Exactly what I was hoping for. I almost tear it open right there on the spot, but I decide to wait instead.

"Look at you," Mother says. "You'd think it was an announcement telling you you've been selected for the national team."

It's not warm outside today, but I can see that the sun's still shining brightly, and that's enough for me. "I think I'm going to take a walk," I announce.

"What about your homework?"

"What about it?"

"Well, do you have any?" Mother asks, her hands on her hips.

"Some," I say.

"Some?"

"Yeah, some."

"And when do you plan to do it?"

I slip on my jacket, grab some nuts from a bowl on the dining room table, and say, "I somehow managed just fine not doing any homework for almost three years. I don't think anything will happen if this batch waits a couple more hours."

Mother walks over and puts a wool cap on my head. "Be careful, Misha." Then she rises up on her toes, because I'm finally taller than her, and kisses me on the cheek. "You'll be back soon, yes?"

"Of course," I say and head out into the hallway.

A couple of blocks from our building, I see Marietta. She's walking with some boy I don't know. She doesn't appear to be terribly happy to see me.

"Hey," I say to her.

"Hey," she says. We stare at each other awkwardly for a few seconds.

"How was school?" she asks.

"Okay," I say, "not bad."

I look over at the boy she's with. He's pretty tall, with very broad shoulders. He smiles a bit and nods once quickly.

"This is Rudi," she says finally.

"Hi," I say.

"This is my brother, Misha."

"Pleasure to meet you," he says, his voice much deeper than I expected.

We stand there a moment longer, then Marietta leans over and whispers, "Don't tell Mother, okay?"

"Okay," I say, and start off walking again. When I turn around a bit later, I see them, walking together in the other direction.

It's not Shabbat, and even if it was I wouldn't be going to the Old-New Synagogue, but that doesn't mean I have anything against the walk Father and I used to take. Especially on a day like today. The trees are mostly bare, but the sun more than makes up for it, and the way it reflects off the river makes me want to whistle.

So I whistle, making up brand-new melodies I should really write down. Though I'd have to learn how to read music first to do that. But who cares? I keep whistling, patting the inside pocket of my jacket every once in a while to make sure the letter hasn't disappeared somehow.

My eyes, of course, wander over to the castle, and then, even though I can't really see it, the Stresovice neighborhood on the far side of it. It's still hard to believe that's where I wound up for a few weeks back in May. One minute Soviet tanks are rolling into the camp, and the next thing I know, that same evening I'm with Zdenek Taussig, one of the great soccer players from Room 1. The two of us, along with his whole family, are riding in a horse-drawn flatbed back to Prague.

Zdenek worked with a couple of old horses in Terezin, plowing fields, taking out garbage, and even moving dead bodies to the crematorium (because they didn't bother to bury us back there). So as soon as the Soviets showed up, Zdenek took his horses and left, pulling his parents, his sister, and their meager possessions on a flatbed. Among those possessions were issues of the magazine *Vedem*, published by the boys in Room 1. Since Zdenek had been the only boy left in Room 1, he had buried the issues and then later dug them up. I hope someday people get to read them.

Mother, not wanting me in that rotten place a second longer, asked Zdenek's father if I could go with them. He agreed. We traveled all night, the skinny horses clop-clopping along like we were just out for a fun moonlit ride. And then, if that weren't crazy enough, Zdenek and I slept in some stables when we got to Prague. We did that for a few days until his family could find an apartment.

Only, little did Mother know that soon after I left, the whole camp would be quarantined because of typhoid. Thankfully, Zdenek's family let me stay with them for a bunch of weeks until Mother and Marietta were finally allowed to leave Terezin. I guess it only makes sense that my two and a half unbelievable years in Terezin would have an ending as strange as that.

I reach the Cechuv Bridge and turn onto it. The wind blows stronger here, but I don't mind, because I decide this is my new ritual. Whenever Franta sends me a letter, this is where I'll read it.

So I walk halfway down the bridge, remembering how I used to secretly race people here when I was younger. But not anymore. Now it's enough just to watch them. Driving their new cars or wearing their new hats or walking in their new shoes. I'm still getting used to it, Prague in 1945. Thankfully the Germans and the Allies didn't bomb it.

I slowly walk until I get to the very middle, to the spot where you can't tell which end is closer. Which also happens to be the spot offering the best view of the castle. A bunch of the Nesharim used to say that after the war we'd meet right here, on this very bridge. But I come here all the time, and haven't seen any of the other boys yet. I'll keep coming, even though I know it's unlikely I'll ever see any of them again. For people our age, transports meant gas.

Gas, then chimney. That's how they killed us, and that's how they got rid of our bodies. I don't know why exactly, but I keep finding myself thinking that sentence for some reason: That's how they killed us, and that's how they got rid of our bodies. It just pops up in my head. And even so, part of me still can't really believe it.

I carefully remove the envelope from my jacket, tear it open, remove the letter, and, holding it very carefully, stick the envelope in my back pocket.

Brno, December 14, 1945

Dear Misha!
I read your sincere, powerful letter. I believe I understood what you wrote, and deep in my heart I must admit I'm proud of what I achieved through all my hard work. Nesharim is much more than just a word, it's an idea that survives among a group of friends, an idea that lives on in each one of you, the lucky survivors. But I must tell you, my dear Misha, that you are far from objective in your evaluation of our time in Terezin. You were relatively well off, you were happy to be among all your pals, so you didn't worry so much.

But you mustn't forget: Terezin was a concentration camp through whose gates entered fresh recruits, only to leave later, sentenced to their death. A place where people starved to death, were hanged, and were at the mercy of their oppressors' every whim. By now I'm sure you know some of what went on there, so you know that our home was a small island of calm growth, a place where we forcefully turned our backs on reality and dedicated ourselves to our own interests and our own future with little regard for anything else.

Meanwhile, almost 35,000 people died in Terezin itself, while those who were transported away reached a destination from which very, very few returned. In this regard, I myself am incredibly lucky. I entered Auschwitz, but avoided the gas chambers.

Terezin, with its mighty walls and a beautiful view of the mountains in the distance, was a cruel and terrible place, even after the Nazis turned it into a show camp, a propaganda tool for the Red Cross. I am glad you didn't feel your shackles to the extent so many others did, but when you write "How I wish those times with the Nesharim might return," I must reply, "How I wish those times will never return." I certainly hope you'll have equally memorable and positive experiences again some day, only outside that bitter prison.

Are such experiences possible? Perhaps.

I imagine that in a summer camp, or even among a group of close friends, a similar environment might be created. Of course, young people like you will never again be linked together so closely and be so dependent on one another as you were back in Terezin. I remember the first weeks in our home, the lack of unity, the impossible variety of personalities, and the way the parents' interference hindered our development. Back then nobody understood that the only way for Room 7 to discover its own needs and to develop its own interests would be by limiting parental involvement. This is how and why our solidarity grew.

These days parents bring their children to summer camp with only the interest of their own children in mind. They don't trust even those people whose task it is to lead their children. Maybe new youth groups will soon emerge again, made up of individuals as dedicated as you yourself. It is such a pity, my boys could have done so many things, but as I tell myself every day, such thinking is in vain.

Eighty boys lived in Room 7 at one point or

another. Eleven survived. Which compared to Terezin as a whole, is an incredible success story. And, of course, Terezin, compared to Auschwitz (and Terezin was little more than a holding pen for Auschwitz, as we all now know)—well, Misha, I'm not sure the two should even be compared.

The promise that we won't forget—I hope you feel it in these lines. The best way to commit to fulfilling the Nesharim legacy would be to fulfill all the things I believed, and still believe, about you. You're capable of all that and so much more, there's no reason to think otherwise. And don't worry, I'm sure we'll manage to meet in person, sooner or later. I look forward to it, but fear it a little as well. I suppose I love the Nesharim a bit too much.

My dear Misha, the coming New Year will mean the end of a chapter in our great adventure. In front of us lies a wide-open space bursting with great possibilities and even greater responsibilities. Turn the page, it's okay. It's doesn't mean you're being disloyal, it doesn't mean you're forgetting the past. You'll continue to remember, and as you do so you'll summon the courage to face the rest of your life. Because it's true, life is a struggle.

Please promise me you won't ever give up.
Best wishes for the New Year.
Yours,
Franta

P.S. Give my best regards to your mother and sister. I'll be sure to let you know when I'm coming to Prague, where we'll finally get to see one another again.

I read the letter two more times, hearing Franta's voice in my head a little more clearly each time. I argue with him a little, but mainly as a way to slowly accept that once again just about everything he has to say is true.

When I finally look up, I'm a bit surprised to find myself standing in the middle of a bridge in the middle of Prague. For a moment I have no idea where to go or what to do. Both ends of the bridge are the same distance from me. There's too much to do, too much to see, and I suddenly feel a strange, overwhelming obligation to live some sort of perfect life, one packed with heroic acts so incredible I can't even begin to imagine what they might be.

I look out at the castle, listen to the birds, feel the wind on my face. It's the same wind that's sending ripples over the surface of the river. The late afternoon air is quite cold, but I don't mind. Winter is coming, but I don't mind that, either.

I take out the envelope, put the letter back inside, carefully return the envelope to my pocket, and start walking back home again. I'm almost six years behind in school, which is a lot to be behind when you're already fifteen years old. So here's my great, heroic plan: I'll finish all my homework, every last bit of it, before dinner.

And after that, who knows?

Afterword by Todd Hasak-Lowy

WHENEVER I SEE A MOVIE THAT OPENS with the words "Based on a true story" or "Inspired by real events," I always wonder: Just how true is this movie, really? If only a handful of events in the movie actually happened, would they still put those words on the screen? And if the movie is only "inspired" by real events, does that mean that the whole movie—from the hero to the setting to maybe even the climax—might be very, very different from the real person, setting, and climax that inspired them?

I wish movies answered these questions, because it matters whether or not something is true. If it didn't, the people who make movies wouldn't put those words on the screen to begin with. We watch, read, and listen to stories differently when we think they actually happened. I even think we value stories more if we believe they're real, which is probably why people who make movies like to open them with "based on a true story" in the first place.

So how true is this book you just read? Is it merely "based" on a true story? Is it just "inspired" by real events?

I think it's more than either of those. Much more, in fact. But to answer these questions fully, I need to explain how this book was written, and why I wrote it the way I did.

After I agreed to write Michael Gruenbaum's story, I traveled from Chicago (where I live) to Boston (where Michael lives). We spent a couple of days together. He told me about his experiences back then and took me to meet a local couple who were in Terezin as well. I asked him a bunch of questions, recorded a lot of what he said, and left Boston with a stack of books and DVDs about Terezin and the Jews of Prague.

When I got back home, I started reading and watching the things Michael had given me. I bought additional books and tracked down additional movies. I began putting together a timeline of the key events in his story. I also sent Michael all sorts of questions—big questions and little questions, easy questions and impossible questions—that I didn't think to ask him when we were together. I tried to figure out what kind of boy Michael might have been seventy years ago, going so far as putting together a questionnaire for

Michael, where I asked him to rate himself on a one-to-ten scale about everything from how neat or sloppy he was as a kid (he rated himself seven, or pretty sloppy) to whether or not he was one, a follower, or ten, a leader (he gave himself a three on that one).

Unfortunately, there was a lot Michael didn't remember about that time. Not because his memory isn't so great in general, not at all. I imagine Michael didn't remember so much in large part because these things happened a long, long time ago, when he was a boy. This makes sense, because, honestly, how much do you really remember about last summer? You probably remember certain days and certain moments, but you've probably forgotten a ton already too. I bet there are entire days you can't recall anymore. Now imagine that last summer was actually seventy summers ago.

It's possible, too, that Michael didn't remember certain events because these experiences were so extremely unpleasant. Psychologists claim that people do this all the time. We forget difficult experiences in order to protect ourselves from the pain of remembering them. I have no idea if this is the case with Michael, and I never asked him if he thinks it is. But for whatever reasons, Michael couldn't remember many things, and I soon understood that even if I wrote down every detail he did remember, I'd still only have maybe twenty or thirty pages of memories. That meant I'd have to fill in the gaps in his memory, either by consulting other sources (people, books, etc.) or elaborating on the fragments of his memories until they became full-fledged scenes.

A couple of weeks after I met Michael, I felt the time had come to start writing. I wasn't sure yet when exactly the story would open, so I decided to write about the day Michael (along with his mother and sister) left Prague for Terezin. I chose this event because I knew this was one of the more surprising moments in Michael's story. In contrast to what I figured anyone would feel about such a move, Michael recalls being relieved to leave his hometown for a concentration camp he knew almost nothing about. He felt this way because of how bad things had gotten for Jews in Prague. But when I sat down to write this scene, I was paralyzed. I was still trying to figure out who Michael the boy was, and even though I knew that he and his family—on that day—were walking from some collection center to the train (and carrying all the possessions they had left in a few bags), the whole scene still felt way too vague to me. I just couldn't see it. What did the buildings they passed look like? What part of the city did they walk through? How big was the train station? I had no idea, and I started getting rather nervous that I wouldn't be able to write anything worth reading until I answered these questions and a bunch more like them.

Then I got lucky. It just so happened that I was scheduled to go to London in a few weeks. I decided I would add a short trip to Prague, a city I had never before visited. And I would spend a day in Terezin as well, which is less than an hour from Prague by car. This might be one of the smartest decisions I've ever made. I walked all over Prague, visiting the places Michael lived, the synagogue he once attended, and that train station his family headed to on their way to Terezin. I even took the exact walk he and his father would take each week from the Holesovice neighborhood to the Old-New Synagogue across the river. And, fortunately for me, Terezin still looks a great deal like it looked back then. I took a ton of pictures, bought some maps, and jotted down my impressions. Suddenly the story began to come alive for me. Before I even left Prague, I started writing—over a plate of Czech dumplings in a restaurant across the street from where I would later imagine Michael sneaking out of the Ghetto to see a matinee—what became the opening scene of this book.

When I returned to Chicago, I consulted (as I continued to expand) my timeline, and simply began writing the chapters in the order they came. Often, in order to write a chapter, I had to ask Michael additional questions, read from this or that book, snoop around the Internet, or do some combination of all these things. My questions for

Michael were now much more specific ("Do you remember if the Old Town Square was within the Jewish Ghetto?"), and sometimes these kinds of pointed questions actually helped him remember things he had forgotten for decades. The more books I read on Terezin, the more I learned about other books out there that could help me, including a diary kept by one of the other Nesharim (Pavel "Pajik" Weiner), which proved crucial. As I sent Michael early drafts, once again he remembered certain incidents and events that he had not mentioned to me before. Michael would often forward questions he himself couldn't answer to other people who had been in Terezin with him. Slowly my picture of Terezin came into sharper and sharper focus until I felt like a genuine expert on the subject.

On occasion there were still things I couldn't reconstruct as much as I wished I could. For example, Michael and his family were placed on but somehow got off a transport just a few days before the decisive October twelfth transport. In some cases, especially if I felt something, in general, needed to be included, we made an educated guess (such as where Michael lived after Franta left and Room 7 was disbanded). But sometimes—like with that other transport—we didn't include it at all, because there was just too much about it we didn't know.

In the end, every chapter here is either the reconstruction of a specific, one-time event that really happened (Michael's father being taken away by two SS officers, Michael being chased and tied up by boys in Prague, Michael seeing his best friend for the last time through the infirmary window) or the creation of a new scene that describes experiences Michael had on more than one occasion (working in the garden, playing soccer on the bashta, learning something from Franta). There isn't a single significant event in this book that I made up just because I thought it might be interesting. Even Franta's letter from the epilogue is real, though I should mention that I added a few details (facts about how many Nesharim and Jews in general survived Terezin) in order to work in some crucial information into this otherwise real document.

That being said, there were still many gaps I had to fill in. For instance, almost every word of dialogue in this book is re-created, something that is the case with just about any memoir. Though the names (and ultimate fates) of all the Nesharim are real (with the exception of Jiri, whom I created myself, since Michael could no longer recall the name or identity of the actual friend he lost there), I had to supply large parts of their personalities and actions in order to bring the scenes with them to life. And there are thousands of other small details scattered all over the book that I had to provide so that this narrative would consistently have the kind of three-dimensionality Michael's story required and deserved. But when I had to guess—what someone wore or ate or even said—I made an educated guess, and after all my research and discussion with Michael, I was pretty highly educated.

But the external world of this story is really only half the book. The other half is Michael's internal world—what he thought and felt about everything. If you connected with this book, I'm guessing the precise way Michael experienced and narrated these events had a lot to do with it. In other words, reading this book isn't just learning what happened to Michael, it's also learning what it might have been like *to be Michael* while all this was happening. Only Michael didn't really narrate these events as they were happening seventy years ago (and even if he had, it certainly wouldn't have been in English!). This means that I may be more responsible for Michael the narrator (the narrator who narrates in present tense as things are happening) than just about anything else in this book. But here, too, I worked off what I thought Michael might have been like back then, even though in the end I had to construct a new Michael who could, in a sense, go through these events all over again.

So why didn't we just have Michael tell his story in

his own voice today, as a bunch of memories he now has? Why didn't the publisher want that kind of book (a much more conventional memoir), which would then, perhaps, have been touched up a bit by me, the professional writer? In writing this book the way I wrote it, I was aiming for immediacy. I wanted to give the reader the experience of going through these events with Michael as Michael goes through them himself. This is why Michael narrates in present tense. I thought a book like that would make the events more powerful, more vivid, and more alive. I thought this would best capture the truth of what it was like to have these experiences, and Michael and the publisher agreed.

I think this is an especially valuable exercise for the reader when it comes to the Holocaust. In the seventy years since those horrible events, people have published thousands and thousands of books on the topic, made thousands of movies on the topic, and asked thousands of survivors to tell their stories over and over again. This is important, and it's a very good and necessary thing overall. But as everyone knows, the more you tell a story, the more it grows apart from the original event itself. Think about some crazy story you've told a bunch of times. After a while, the story hardens into its own thing, until you're not really remembering what happened, you're remembering your story about the thing.

I didn't want this book to read like a story about the Holocaust, I wanted it to read like a person living through those events at that time. For that reason, Michael the narrator doesn't really know he's narrating at all, the reader is just somehow getting the words that surface in his head at that time. Sure, sometimes the words might be beautiful or a little poetic, but what do you want from me—I'm a writer.

There is another reason I wrote this book this way. In the case of the Holocaust, we write a lot of these books and tell a lot of these stories in order to educate all the people who didn't go through it themselves. We want to educate people not just about what happened, but how something so unimaginably horrible could have happened, all so we might prevent something like this from ever happening again. This is also a very important thing to do, to tell a story in order to encourage people to behave in a particular way in their own lives.

But this wasn't really my goal here, even though I know (and hope) that teachers might use this book to discuss all these important topics. My goal here was simply to re-create what it might have been like for a pretty regular boy to go through these extremely irregular experiences. Michael didn't know that later on we'd have all sorts of terms ("survivor," "death camp," even "Holocaust" itself) to describe and name these events. He didn't know that his experiences might be retold someday in order to educate people about what happened, all so we might prevent such a thing from happening again. Michael was simply going through it, moment by unbelievable moment. And so my goal here was simply to re-create those moments, and make Michael's experiences of them as immediate, as vivid, and, in a certain sense, as *real* as possible.

I firmly believe that this approach was the right one for this story, but that doesn't mean it didn't come at a cost. There were certain real events that couldn't be included in this book, because including them would have meant breaking the rule regarding what Michael knew at the time. The most glaring example of this has to do with how Michael's father was killed. If you read the book closely, all you learned is that he was arrested, taken to a prison in Prague, and then sent to the Small Fortress at Terezin, where he died within two weeks. The reader never learns for certain how he died, though it seems clear that the reason provided by the Nazis (uremia, a type of kidney failure) was not the real reason. In addition, during the funeral itself, one of Michael's uncles—disregarding a warning sent along with the casket itself—looks at the corpse and is horrified by what he sees. Otherwise that's it.

The truth is that eventually Michael would learn with some certainty how his father died, and it's a truly terrible story. A woman who lived with his mother and sister at Terezin wrote a letter that Michael would see years later. The crucial part of it reads:

> A *former director of a well-known banking firm, whose wife and daughter are both living in my room, was literally torn to pieces in the "small fortress" by dogs trained precisely for this purpose by the SS.*

The unimaginable brutality of this killing is, understandably, a truth that's deeply important to Michael, and so it's no surprise that he very much wanted it included in the book. Unfortunately, it was clear to me that not only didn't Michael know this at the time, but that his mother (who clearly *did* know about it then, since she was able to tell the woman who wrote this letter) intentionally hid it from him, most likely to protect him from the pain of such knowledge. We considered pretending this wasn't the case in order to include it, but ultimately concluded that doing so would require not just breaking the rule but, just as important, following the aftereffects of Michael learning this throughout the rest of the book. Learning the truth would have, in other words, changed his entire experience of being in Terezin in a meaningful way. For these reasons, we chose to leave it out.

I should mention one last thing, a confession actually: I didn't want to work on this project when I was first given the opportunity. I had read many books about the Holocaust myself—not to mention seen the movies, been to the museums, and listened to the survivors. I had, I guess, started to mistake all those stories—told over and over again—for the thing itself. This mistake somehow almost caused me to forget that all these stories are about absolutely real things that happened to absolutely real people. I don't feel good about this, but it's true. Or maybe I shouldn't be so hard on myself. After all, how is one supposed to make dinner or give his daughter a bath or go to work while remembering what really and truly happened in Europe from 1939 to 1945?

Writing this book helped me to remember. Trying to imagine what it might have been like to be Michael Gruenbaum during those years allowed me to see, almost for the first time again, what it must have truly been like. This wasn't the "Holocaust" anymore, this was simply a boy watching his world, bit by bit, steadily transform from something close to a paradise into an unbelievable nightmare. This was a boy laughing and kicking around a soccer ball with his new friends one day and watching them disappear the next. It's my hope that this book might allow its readers to have a similar experience, however painful that may be. Because, it's true, all this actually happened.

Acknowledgments

I WISH TO ACKNOWLEDGE MY FATHER, Dr. Karl Grünbaum, and especially my mother, Mrs. Margaret Gruenbaum, for not only giving me my life, but saving it on numerous occasions during the most perilous times during World War II and having the wisdom and energy to make us emigrate from Czechoslovakia and start a new life in the United States shortly after the end of the war. My mother has been a beacon to me as I reflect on how she overcame incredible difficulties during her lifetime, always having a positive attitude and teaching me never to give up in the pursuit of my goals. At the same time, I wish to thank my sister, Marietta, for helping my mother take good care of me and always being on the ready to help me when such help was needed, especially during the trying days during World War II.

I also wish to acknowledge my late wife, Thelma Gruenbaum, for her encouragements during fifty years of a most wonderful and loving partnership and for researching and writing the splendid book *Nešarim: Child Survivors of Terezín*, which helped solidify the team spirit of the small number of Nesharim survivors. In addition, her love for children and music and her striving for excellence resulted in a very successful upbringing of our three sons.

Additionally, I wish to acknowledge the enthusiastic support of our sons, David, Peter, and Leon Gruenbaum, for all the projects I have been involved in during my lifetime, and especially the development of this particular book. I am very proud of their individual achievements and their contributions to make this world a much better place.

I want to thank Ms. Ava Farber for her help in writing the original children's book. I also want to thank all the Nesharim for their camaraderie, and especially Erich Spitz, George Repper, and Paul Weiner for helping me remember some of the details of our stay in Terezin. I want to thank Franta Maier—not only for his leadership and care under very trying circumstances in Terezin, but also for his interest in the lives of the survivors of Room 7 in the school building L417 in Terezin throughout the remainder of his life. I want to thank Sidney Taussig and his family for transporting me with them from Terezin to Prague and for providing accommodations for me for several weeks until my mother was allowed to leave Terezin when the typhoid quarantine was finally lifted. I also want to thank Tommy Karas for his deep friendship, Judith Cohen of the Holocaust Museum in Washington DC for her interest and initiatives in bringing my mother's album of important Terezin documents to the attention of the public, and to my friend Mimi Dohan for her continued encouragement and support.

Finally, I wish to thank Ms. Amy Berkower, my literary agent, for always being there when help was needed, as well as to several staff members from Simon & Schuster: Ms. Karen Nagel and Ms. Liesa Abrams for their editorial acumen and Ms. Mara Anastas and Ms. Fiona Simpson for their enthusiastic support and expert guidance. I also wish to thank Ms. Fern Schumer Chapman for helping me turn my memoirs into prose and Ms. Bethany Buck for recognizing the intrinsic value of my story and for her excellent selection of Todd Hasak-Lowy to be my coauthor. I was amazed to see him immerse himself so completely and with such great imagination into the life of a twelve-year-old during the Nazi occupation in Prague and later in Terezin and to address constructive criticism with a very positive attitude; I think he did a terrific job, and it was truly a great pleasure to work with him.

—Michael Gruenbaum

I'd like to thank the following people, who helped me reconstruct the world in which this story takes place: Fern Schumer Chapman, David Gruenbaum, Peter Gruenbaum, Leon Gruenbaum, Petr Karas, the late Tommy Karas, Ivana Králová, Edgar Krasa, Hana Krasa, Vida Neuwirthová, George Repper, Erich Spitz, and Ela Weissberger.

Ron Lowy offered steady, unbridled enthusiasm. Noam Hasak-Lowy and Anna Levy read a full draft and provided valuable, thoughtful feedback.

Thanks to my agent, Daniel Lazar, for approaching me with this project, helping me make sense of what might be involved, and advocating for me throughout. Liesa Abrams, my brilliant, sensitive editor, did a wonderful job, as usual, understanding the potential of this story and figuring out how to realize it.

I'm grateful to Michael Gruenbaum for trusting his story with me. Michael was a pleasure to work with, did an enormous amount of crucial research himself, and helped me make the most of my short trip to Prague and Terezin.

He managed time and again—and in a manner that still mystifies me—to distinguish between himself and his memories, on the one hand, and the needs of this book, on the other.

And, once again, Taal.

—Todd Hasak-Lowy

For those interested in reading more about Terezin, the following is a selected bibliography. Titles with an * will be of special interest to younger readers. You'll notice that this list includes *Vedem*, the Terezin magazine published by boys Michael's age and saved by Zdenek Taussig at the end of the war.

Nešarim: Child Survivors of Terezín, Thelma Gruenbaum

The Terezin Diary of Gonda Redlich, Saul S. Friedman, editor

* *A Boy In Terezín: The Private Diary of Pavel Weiner, April 1944–April 1945*, Pavel Weiner

* *Helga's Diary: A Young Girl's Account of Life in a Concentration Camp*, Helga Weiss

* *The Cat with the Yellow Star: Coming of Age in Terezin*, Ela Weissberger

Ghetto Theresienstadt, Zdenek Lederer

We Are Children Just the Same: Vedem, *the Secret Magazine of the Boys of Terezin*, Paul R. Wilson, editor

About the Authors

MICHAEL GRUENBAUM was born in Prague, Czechoslovakia, in 1930. His father was active in Prague's Jewish community; he and Michael's grandfather held prestigious seats in the famous Altneuschul synagogue. After the Nazis occupied Czechoslovakia in 1939, Michael's father was arrested, tortured, and sent to the Small Fortress in Terezin, where he was killed within two weeks. Michael was sent to Terezin in 1942 with his mother and sister and remained there until the war ended two and a half years later. The family returned to Prague, having lost their relatives, friends, and possessions; they left in April 1948 and spent two years in Cuba before being allowed to enter the United States. In Cuba, Michael, who did not speak English or Spanish, attended an American high school, graduating in two years, in time to enter MIT.

Michael received his BSCE from MIT (Massachusetts Institute of Technology) in three years; he was drafted during the Korean War and spent two years in the army. He worked for the Illinois Highway Department in Chicago and met his wife, Thelma, to whom he was married for fifty years. He earned his master's in city planning at Yale University and worked for the Boston Redevelopment Authority, publishing a book entitled *Transportation Facts for the Boston Region*. He later served as special assistant to the commissioner of the Massachusetts Department of Public Works, worked for a large consulting firm, and eventually helped form a private engineering company where he became a partner. In retirement, Thelma wrote a book about Michael and his friends' experiences called *Nešarim: Child Survivors of Terezín*, which was published in the United Kingdom and is now in its second edition. Unfortunately, Thelma contracted ALS and lost her valiant fight three years later.

Thelma and Michael have three sons, David, Peter, and Leon. Michael still lives in the same house in Brookline, Massachusetts, that he and Thelma moved to more than forty-five years ago. Recently, Michael established a fund at the MIT music library in memory of his parents.

TODD HASAK-LOWY is the author of four books of fiction, including the middle-grade novel *33 Minutes*, also published by Aladdin. Todd holds a PhD in Comparative Literature from the University of California, Berkeley, and was an assistant and later associate professor of Hebrew Language and Literature at the University of Florida from 2002–2010. In 2010 he left his academic position and relocated to Evanston, Illinois, with his wife and two daughters, in order to focus on his creative writing. In addition to writing books, Todd translates Hebrew fiction into English and teaches courses in both Creative Writing and Literature at the School of the Art Institute of Chicago.